Wildlife in North America: Birds

Wildlife in North America: Birds

R. D. Lawrence

CHILTON BOOK COMPANY
RADNOR, PENNSYLVANIA

© R. D. Lawrence 1974

Published in Canada by Thomas Nelson & Sons (Canada) Limited,
81 Curlew Drive, Don Mills, Ontario, M3A 2R1.

Published simultaneously in the United States of America
by Chilton Book Company, Chilton Way, Radnor, Pennsylvania
19089, and in Great Britain by Michael Joseph Limited,
52 Bedford Square, London WC1B 3ES.

ISBN 0-176-39216-5

Library of Congress Catalog Card Number 74-82665

Printed and bound in Canada

234567890MR832109876

To Sharon
whose love and encouragement
make all things possible, this book is
dedicated.

Contents

Preface

This book is written for those who wish to know something about the birds that they are likely to see in their gardens or during some summer outing. It is not intended to be a guide to all the birds of North America. Rather, I have tried to sketch the characters and habits of some of the better-known birds and particularly of those species with which I have personally associated during my rather wide wanderings over this continent.

For the reader who does not already own a guidebook there are numerous aids available, the best of which are undoubtedly Roger Tory Peterson's *Field Guide to the Birds of Eastern North America* and the companion *Field Guide to the Birds of Western North America*.

An excellent reference work for the home library is *The Birds of Canada* by W. Earl Godfrey. Nearly all the birds it describes are common to both the United States and Canada; only those species that are confined to the extreme south are absent from its pages.

It is my hope that readers will find in the pages of *Wildlife in North America: Birds* as much pleasure as I did in meeting the characters of these stories and writing about them.

R. D. Lawrence
Gibson Lake, Ontario
June 1974

Spear Fisherman

At four o'clock on a midsummer morning, the wilderness is a place of vague blue light that outlines the shapes of trees and rocks and etches in velvet the surface of a beaver pond. Overhead the stars are fading quietly. The sounds and movements of night are beginning to give way to those of day, as light seeps slowly into the forest. Mosquitoes drone more softly. Some of the birds are stirring on their perches, emitting small, half-hearted chirps. Perch and catfish poke at the surface of the water in the beaver pond, making little circular waves. As the ripples travel outwards, they greet the things that they encounter, bumping gently into bur-reed and sedge, sliding under some water lily leaf or dancing bit of flotsam. At last, with a faint whisper, they spend themselves against grassy bank or rocky shoreline. The trees speak; evergreens swish as the soft, springing breeze rumples their needles, and aspens shake their heart-shaped leaves.

An hour later, the blue light has gone. The stars have been eclipsed and the light of budding day is like the sheen of burnished steel. There is no sun yet, but the east is rosy-hued in expectation as streaks and spears of color shaft into the empty sky. A beaver rises by his lodge and moves in a straight line for the cat-tail stand on which he was feeding yesterday. A dragonfly hurries on lacy wings in pursuit of a mosquito, and is itself engulfed as it flies within reach of a bullfrog's sticky tongue. A bird sings.

Sitting on a dead stub in the center of the pond, silhouetted against the lightening skyline, a red-winged blackbird greets the day with his bubbling song. He balances precari-

ously as he sings, bowing and spreading his wings and show-ing off his red and yellow epaulets. And now it is true dawn.

The great blue heron flaps lazily as he heads for the beaver pond, his neck forming an S-bend, his long beak opening to emit a hoarse, goose-like sound. *Onk*, cries the stilt-legged bird, for perhaps no more valid reason than to greet the day. Moving in slow motion, he angles towards the pond, long legs swept backwards under his tail. Down he goes, aiming for a shallow area that is littered with old beaver cuttings, some newly peeled and still yellow, others waterlogged and brown, a haven for frogs and catfish.

The heron lets down his legs, back-flaps his great wings to break his landing speed, and alights gracefully in the shal-lows. For a moment the bird ducks down, then rises, shakes his wings and folds them while he looks around, inspecting his surroundings. At his feet, the ooze he has disturbed in landing floats like a cloud of green-brown dye, and bits of rotting leaf and decaying twig come up to the surface. To the life that this bird hunts these are warning signs and the heron knows that he must wait, sentry-still, until the telltale debris has settled again.

The mallards and black ducks have been sheltering in the lee of a large island in the southerly end of the pond. There grow the rushes and sedges, flanked in the deeper water by the water-lilies. The white blooms are still closed, and the yellow flowers of the brandy-bottles shelter tiny black mites that scuttle among the pollen-heavy stamens.

The ducks emerge in flotillas, chatting like gossipy neigh-bors or calling encouragement to their ducklings. A small leopard frog rests on a broad green lily leaf, spread-eagled in the little pool of water that the weight of its body has caused to collect on the upper side of the leaf. A mallard, followed by seven downy ducklings, breaks formation and heads for the frog, and the small amphibian collects his limbs and jumps into the water.

High above the ducks and the pond and the heron and all the other creatures of this wilderness hangs a red-shouldered

---

Great blue heron

hawk, gliding in graceful freedom on his first flight of the day, eagerly scanning the ground for food.

The heron remains unmoving, classifying each sound and noting each sight, aware of the things that are taking place around him and alert for signs of danger. Like all his kind he is a cautious bird, and for that reason he has survived seven years of wilderness living. The ooze at his feet is almost settled and his sharp eyes await the first tiny flicker of movement that will signal the arrival of frog or fish.

He is a four-foot-tall study in still life as the sun slides over the far-off ridge. The new light catches him in profile and shows off the long, glossy plumes that sprout from the back of his head. His blue-gray wings and back contrast with the lighter neck and belly and the white top-knot with its black cap that is like a fringe of hair on a bald man's head. His beak, the long, heavy spear with which he has sustained his life, gleams yellow in the sun. The bird's reflection shows clearly in the quiet water; it is like the heron's twin lying on its side beneath the surface, and is just as still.

The heron sees movement. His big, yellow eyes focus on a place about ten feet away and follow the dim and fluid outlines of a large catfish that is also seeking prey. The brown bullhead swims slowly, now and then stopping to gulp down mouthfuls of bottom debris, from which it extracts tiny morsels of living food. But the bullhead is seeking minnows this morning and must swim to the shallows, where the heron waits. The fish is almost eighteen inches long, and it is fat and broad; it will make a good breakfast for the heron this morning, if the big bird is patient and the fish gets close enough.

So the fish swims and the heron stands motionless. The mallards call and the red-wing quiets his voice and devotes some attention to his tail feathers, spreading them and arranging them fussily with his beak. And the hawk sweeps in wide circles and watches the clearings for squirrel or chipmunk or mouse.

The fish is close, almost within striking distance of the heron. The long neck uncoils slightly, moving the great bill imperceptibly closer to the water, as the bird notes the approach

Herons fly with neck bent back against the body.

of the bullhead. Inches only separate the heron from his meal. The bird waits; the fish, unaware, swims slowly towards its death.

Now! The poised beak flashes forward, and impales the fish. A splash, a swirl, and up comes the heron's spear, the catfish secured. But it is too large to turn and swallow, and it is fighting too hard. The heron moves stiffly towards the shore, lifting his stilt-legs almost woodenly, in a caricature of walking. When he reaches the shore he pounds the catfish to death on a rock, turns it headfirst, and tosses it down his gullet. The fish bulges the heron's throat and the bird swallows harder; down goes the fish, but slowly, and the heron is al-

Heron stalking prey

most gasping for air before he has managed to ingest the bullhead.

At last it is done, and the bird moves back into the water, to stand meditative in the early sun, replete and warm. Perhaps he thinks a little of his young and of his mate back there in the tree, perched on the bulky nest of sticks. He should take some fish to the noisy brood, but he is too full. Later. He will go back later. Now he wants to sleep a little.

Valley of the Eagles

One spring, at break-up time, I was camped on the shores of the Skeena River, in northern British Columbia, studying the early migration of salmon fry. The weather was still cold at night and great blocks of ice trundled groaning down the river towards the Pacific Ocean. Stubborn patches of snow clung to the forested edge of the river, and the scarps of the Coast Mountains gleamed white as they thrust upwards on either side of the deep Skeena valley.

I had been camped for almost a week and had already noted some of the early migratory birds, such as juncos and redwings and fox sparrows, but the area of my campsite had been relatively quiet, with only an occasional raven hanging around the tent looking for handouts. But on the morning of the sixth day, as I emerged from my tent, chilled and thinking only of the warmth of a campfire and a mug of coffee, I noticed what I first thought to be a flock of ravens perching on the ice-blocks up and down the river. I was still bleary-eyed from sleep and was about to start the fire, when suddenly I realized with excitement that the thirty or more birds out there were bald eagles.

They appeared to have arrived overnight and were now busy fishing. Some were actively searching the water for victims, others had evidently already breakfasted to repletion, judging by the sleepy, satisfied way in which they perched. I had never seen so many eagles in one place at one time.

At first I was reluctant to move for fear of frightening the birds, but the cold and my own needs forced me to kindle the fire and make breakfast. To my surprise, my actions and the noise that I was making had little effect on the eagles. By now I had counted them; there were thirty-eight birds out there. Apart from moving some distance away from my campsite, they stayed on, fishing and resting and occasionally flying about making their thin, reedy little calls, and kept me company for the remainder of my stay in that place.

Such a concentration of eagles might never come my way again, I reflected after breakfast, and so I neglected the salmon in favor of the big birds of prey, watching them as they hunted, rested and indulged in pre-nesting courtship flights.

Eagles normally hunt by flying at varying heights over land or water and scanning the area beneath, seeking the movement of their prey, then descending in a dive to grasp fish or bird with their great talons. On the Skeena that spring, the eagles favored another method. Sitting on an ice cake, they scanned the water, then, as a fish swam by, they would dart off their perch and skim over the water, following the fish for a little distance before shooting down their talons and grasping it. When the fish was secured, they flew to ice-floe or bank and ate it. Now and then one or more would resort to the normal hunting technique, flying up and down river and diving on their prey, and it was during one of these maneuvers that an eagle treated me to an unusual and fascinating sight.

I had been watching the bird as it wheeled and glided on its quest and I had seen it swoop down and catch two small fish, perhaps ten-inchers, when it suddenly dived once more and hooked into a fish so large that it could not lift it out of the water. Now, I thought, the bird will drown, for most birds of prey, once they have activated their grasp, cannot let go until they reach solid footing again. Many a fish-eating eagle has been pulled under and drowned by its intended victim.

But on this occasion, and to my utter amazement, the eagle, after some frantic wing-flapping, proceeded literally to row itself ashore with its wings, sculling in great flaps that propelled it swiftly to the riverbank. As soon as it had dragged its prey to the shallows, it stopped, bent its head and grasped the large ling-cod with its beak. The fish was, by ac-

Bald eagle

---

tual measurement, thirty-two inches long and, alive and whole, must have weighed a good thirty pounds. The eagle dragged its catch to shore and ate about a third of it, then flapped away to settle on a tall fir. I walked to the fish, measured it and, lacking scales, lifted it to estimate its weight.

Every morning and evening I counted the eagles. I noted that each day one or more pairs would be gone, no doubt to carry on with the business of nesting and raising the young. On my last day by the Skeena, nineteen birds still remained, but I was sure that they, too, would soon be gone, for the ice had now vanished and spring had really arrived.

Bald eagles were once relatively common right across Canada and the United States, but hunting and pesticides have thinned the numbers of these great birds to a trickle throughout most of eastern North America. The birds are still plentiful on the west coast, where they range as far north as Alaska and the Bering Sea. They live mainly on fish and carrion, and some smaller birds such as gulls and terns.

Pairs of these great birds usually stay together until one or the other of them dies, and they generally occupy the same nest every year, adding each spring to the untidy structure of sticks and branches on a cliffside or high in the crotch of a tall tree. In this great heap of a nest the mother eagle lays from one to three dull white eggs which seem small for a bird that measures up to three feet in length and has a wing-span of almost seven feet.

The parent birds take turns to sit on the eggs, which hatch in about thirty-five days, and they likewise share in the duties of raising the downy youngsters. These grow rapidly. At a month they are still clothed in tight down from which pro-trude the growing feathers, and by then they are almost as large as their parents. At six weeks, the young eagles are ful-ly fledged, but have not yet learned to fly. Not until about twelve weeks of age do the young take to the air.

At this time the birds are dark brown all over, for the char-acteristic white head and tail of the species will not be fully developed until they are about four years old.

Although it is about the same size as the bald eagle, per-haps somewhat bigger, the golden eagle is easily distin-guished from its white-headed relative by its brown coloring and, when visible, the feathers it wears on its legs right down to the toes. Inexperienced observers might at first mistake a juvenile bald eagle for the golden, but, in flight anyway, the young eagle shows light patches on the forward edges of its wings. Immature golden eagles often have a white tail and white patches at the ends of the wings, but the tail ends in a broad black band, unlike the pure white tail of the adult bald eagle.

The golden eagle nests usually on cliff ledges, sometimes in trees, making a large, bulky nest out of sticks and bark and lining it with mosses, grasses, weeds and leaves. As a rule, the female lays two eggs, though three are not unusual, and the young do not hatch for about forty-three days.

Golden eagle

The parents must spend much of their time scouting the countryside for food to take back to the young, often flying high and scanning the ground with eyes that are capable of spotting a mouse from a distance of 400 feet or more. Although small mammals, such as mice, rabbits, marmots and ground squirrels, furnish the bulk of its diet it will also attack birds such as crows and magpies, and may pick off a lamb or two if it gets the chance.

Perhaps because it must exercise greater patience and alertness in order to obtain food, the golden eagle is much more wary than the bald eagle and it will shy away from an observer while still some distance off. This eagle is also reputed to be of a fiercer disposition and has been known to attack a human if its nest is disturbed.

The golden eagle is a native of Europe and Asia as well as North America, ranging far south in mountainous country. While it usually inhabits the mountains and foothills, it will sometimes be found hunting over the plains. In our continent it occurs mainly in the far west, from Alaska south to Mexico, having almost disappeared from its former ranges in the east.

Although the golden eagle is not yet considered to be an endangered species, the numbers of these birds are declining drastically. For years, eagles have been shot, poisoned and trapped by ranchers who resent the bird's attacks upon their stock, even though, in actual fact, the eagle does far more good than harm by keeping down the rodent populations on these same ranches. And now these magnificent birds, like all predators, are the recipients of cumulative doses of pesticides, such as DDT, from the chain of life upon which they depend.

Cock-of-the-North

The cock-of-the-north is drumming. Looking as though he were glued to the smooth wood of a dead elm, the big woodpecker is assaulting the rotting tree with his powerful beak, telling the forest and his rivals that he has claimed this piece of wilderness for his own. Below the crow-sized bird lies the beaver swamp and perhaps two dozen more dead, barkless trees. A beaver, swimming placidly from his lodge, is startled by the barrage of powerful strokes the woodpecker is dealing to the tree. He is an old beaver and he knows from past experience where the drumming is coming from and who is making it, but, perhaps because age has made him crusty, he slams his broad tail atop the water, supplying one great, resounding crack of his own before he quietly sinks below the dark surface. The cock-of-the-north pauses in his assault on the tree, looks down, notes the swirl where the beaver has dived and shifts his grip on the elm, moving up a little. At the same time he peers around, making sure that the female he is courting is still watching and listening. She is. She sits on a stark branch, intent on the male's solo.

The pileated woodpecker resumes his drumming. This is just noise-making at which he is engaged, akin to the drumming of the ruffed grouse, a courting display intended to woo the hen and to tell other pileated males that he will defend this swamp area to the death if he has to. And because he is not excavating for ants, no chips are falling to the water, for his blows are direct, intended only to create the drum rolls that echo through the forest.

Now the female flies over to the same tree. She lands

against it, her strong, yoked toes, two in front and two at the rear of each foot—like most of the woodpeckers, but unlike most other birds, which have three toes in front and one behind—grip the wood, her bristly tail with the heavy feather shafts pressing against the wood and acting as further support. She pecks tentatively at the tree, two or three half-hearted blows that produce only a muted sound. The male becomes excited and redoubles his efforts, smashing again and again at the tree and filling the wilderness with his strange love song.

Several feet below the two birds, there is an oval hole some five inches wide at the middle which they excavated last year. It will be used again this spring after the two have mated, when the female will lay three to four white eggs within the cavity. Eighteen days after the two birds begin incubating the eggs, the young will hatch.

Just now, though, the pair are more intent on courtship and food than on egg-laying and incubation. The male stops drumming to call, his *whucker, whucker, whucker* flicker-like in tone, but louder and slower. The female answers him, and as they fly off into the deep woods the early sunlight flashes on their black and white bodies and blood-red crests, and picks out the male's fine red moustache.

The male lands on a leaning jack pine, flapping his wings a couple of times to get his balance. Then he begins to slither up and down and around the scaly trunk, listening, now and then probing experimentally with his great beak. He finds a likely place and begins to pound in earnest. Bark and yellow chips quickly begin to fly and the sound of his pecking, though quite different to the tone of his earlier drumming, is yet powerful.

The female has landed in an adjacent tree and she, too, has found a place where the big black carpenter ants are tunneling within the dying wood. Soon both birds are pounding and the large oblong holes take shape. Always, it seems, the pileated woodpecker makes his holes oval or oblong, unlike other woodpeckers, the lesser ones, who are content to peck out roundish holes. Why the pileated has developed this

---

Pileated woodpecker

shape to its digging is not clear, though it may be that because of the larger head and longer beak, this kind of excavation allows the big logger-bird to reach its food more easily.

The two birds continue pecking and feeding as first one, then the other, breaks through into a colony of insects. The power of their blows fills the forest with sound.

In the area of their home range, other diseased trees bear testimony of the cock-of-the-north's work. The workings are easily visible, some old and now occupied by squirrel or by flicker or some other kind of bird; others fresh and yellow, weeping sap, while the forest floor below is littered with wood chips. In places, trees that were weakened by the ants or beetles have been holed by the woodpeckers and, as a result of further weakening, have fallen. Now they are slowly rotting, adding their remains to the humus of the forest floor and giving sanctuary to a number of living things.

The big birds have finished their meal. They fly off into the forest to rest and to make ready for the nesting time. It is afternoon; the sun is westering. In the distance a loon calls, is answered by another. Then the forest is quiet.

The Listeners

The cabin nestles in the woods and overlooks a small lake. It is a place where we go to escape the summer city, to do some physical work—for the building is far from finished—and where we relax. In between digging out foundations again so as to remove rather vast amounts of porcupine debris, stripping down that old dresser to the bare wood and patching the holes where white-footed mice have effected entry, my wife and I like to listen to the birds, and to watch them, of course, during the day. Then, at evening, the young raccoon comes along to the feeding station by the birch cluster and looks over the tidbits we have put out for him. As I go outside to handfeed him, a whip-poor-will calls and a nighthawk strums with his wings as he dives after emitting his nasal call.

It is a pleasant retreat, marred only by the presence of "our nearest neighbor" who, in all fairness, was there first and who feels that he has seniority. He is a chap given to moods and whimsies whom we occasionally see as he stomps about among his trees frowning and, I maintain, attempting to crush the wildflowers in order to relieve his frustrations. This is as it may be, and, in any event, we seem to have reached a sort of armed truce which reveals itself by the studious way in which we ignore one another. Such is the way of *Homo sapiens!*

All of which brings me to an incident that took place one spring. It was Friday and we had arrived early, unpacked our goods from the car and trudged them to the cabin, for we do not yet have a road into our sanctum. We had supper and

Hairy Woodpecker

drank tea and relaxed, enjoying a beautiful early evening and watching the blackburnian warblers as they flitted from branch to branch in their assiduous search for insects.

I was admiring the orange flashes on the face, head and chest of a male blackburnian while my wife was clearing the supper table. Suddenly, from the end of the cabin nearest to the domain of "our nearest neighbor" came a loud banging. It was regular, each knock spaced. It sounded like someone smashing at the outside wall with a hammer, and because the cabin was still a shell on the inside the reverberations were astounding. My wife looked at me, startled. I made some unprintable comments about "the idiot next door" and headed out, blood in my eye, ready to do battle.

I was just taking a purposeful step around the corner of the building when the barrage of blows started up again. But this time it was "woodpecker normal"! Instantly I knew that the hairy woodpecker that had been prospecting our small estate during the last three weeks had decided to claim the territory for himself and was using our cabin as his sounding post. Doubtless he was delighted that he had found this oddly-shaped "tree" that gave out such a resounding and satisfying echo.

As we got over our amusement—I feeling a little sheepish because I had so quickly and belligerently jumped to conclusions—I reflected that this was the first time I had experienced the sensations that must be felt by an insect when a woodpecker assaults the tree in which the pest is hiding! But it was not the first time that a woodpecker had used my dwelling for his courting ritual—and it wasn't the last.

Ten minutes later, the hairy was back again. He kept up the pounding until I picked up an axe-handle and pounded right back, at which he let out a startled *kuk* and flew away. Fine, I thought; I had established my own claim to the "drumming tree".

Not a bit of it. At precisely five-twenty the next morning, my wife and I were awakened by the woodpecker's novel alarm. I staggered sleepily into the living room, seized the axe-handle once more and thumped so hard it is a wonder I didn't knock out the wall. Again the *kuk* sound from the bird and he left. Back to bed and we turned over and snoozed. But only for an hour. Once more our sleep was shattered by the drumming. We gave up and left our bed and, seemingly satisfied with his morning's work, the woodpecker went about his business.

For two weeks that bird drummed on our cabin at intervals, beginning between five and five-thirty in the morning and saving one last stentorian tattoo for evening. Then, presumably, having warned off all other questing males in the area and found his lady-love for that year, he settled down to the business of raising another family of tree pounders.

The uninitiated may wonder how a bird no bigger than a small robin can have the strength to pound so loudly on, and to chisel so efficiently in, a tree; and so did I, until an unfortunate downy woodpecker broke its neck by flying against one of our window panes. I dissected that bird and was struck with the development of its neck muscles and the thickness and strength of the bones of its skull. I noted, too, its sharp, chisel-shaped bill, a most effective tool for excavating wood.

Another very special feature possessed by the woodpecker is its tongue, which is very long and can be extended an inch or two beyond the tip of its bill. In addition, it is coated with sticky saliva and is armed at its tip with a number of backward-sloping barbs. After the bird has drilled a hole and has reached the colony of insects that infest the tree, the elastic tongue shoots out and the insects that are not impaled by its hard point or by its barbs, get mired on its sticky surface.

The tongues of woodpeckers are modified according to their feeding habits of the various species. The sapsucker drills little holes in the bark of trees, about one-quarter inch in diameter, and licks up the flowing sap. Its tongue is equipped with bristles instead of barbs, rather like a bottle brush; these bristles take up sap by capillary action. Later the bird returns to the tree and eats the ants and other insects that have been attracted to the sap oozing from the shallow holes it has made.

The flicker's tongue has few barbs and is longer than the tongue of a hairy woodpecker. It, too, is coated with sticky saliva and as the bird struts along the ground, rooting out the ants that compose more than half of its diet, the insects stick to its tongue. The flicker also consumes other insects, small nuts, and a little wild fruit.

In addition to all these features, woodpeckers appear to be able to hear their insect prey moving within the tree. Watching a woodpecker as it hammers at a tree, an observer will note that the bird first taps at a branch or trunk a few times, rapidly, then lifts its head and adopts a listening attitude. I have observed this behavior many times and have noted that sometimes the bird quickly moved away, either to begin again on another part of the tree or to fly to another tree. It seems likely that the reason for this change of location was

Yellow-bellied sapsucker

Tyrants of the Air

A dull brown bird with gray-white chest and stomach and a long bobbing tail sits on the swaying branch of a young poplar that grows beside the stream. He balances easily, keeping time with his tail to the wind-sway of his perch, wagging it up and down. The bird is bright-eyed—perky, some might say—and in the sunlight his small black beak shines like the tip of a burnished lance.

An insect crawls out from among last year's leaves on the stream bank, spreads its chitinous wing-covers, and rises into the air. The ground beetle, though a graceless flier, is swift and it quickly passes within fifteen feet of the perching bird.

The bird spots the beetle. He opens his beak and calls once, *fee-be*, accenting the first syllable. In a flash of brown wings and spread tail he leaves the branch, maneuvers rapidly a few times and snaps up the flying beetle. On the wing the phoebe swallows his catch, and goes back to his perch. There he utters a rapid call which, though simple, is sweet and melodious. As his voice stills, an answering call reaches him. The female flies swiftly into view and alights in her mate's tree. The two birds sway and balance and bob their tails, repeating their two-syllabled calls again and again.

Spring has brought the phoebes back to this place where they mated and nested last year, building their mud and grass cup on a ledge underneath the little bridge that spans the stream. Here the pair will nest again and they will raise their brood of four or five after the hen bird lays her white eggs on a bed of moss and fine grasses within the mud cup. But first they must rebuild, for winter's cold and snows and the rains of early spring have crumbled the edges of the nest and filled its hollow with debris.

Just now, though, the phoebes are taking their leisure. They have had a long flight from the Gulf of Mexico and since their arrival yesterday they have been feeding and courting and indulging themselves. Now and then the timbre of their call changes, losing its sweetness and taking on a more irritable note. At these times, the accent falls on the second syllable—*fe-bee*—an impatient little sound. Then comes a sharp *chip* as though one of the birds had begun to sound its usual call and had changed its mind.

In today's sunshine, the phoebes show by action and sound that they are happy to be back home in this place where the insects abound and the shelter is good and there is not too much competition from others of their kind, or even from other species. They fuss over each other. The male preens his mate, gently, nibbling at the feathers on the back of her dark brown head, and she coyly accepts his affections, bending to his beak. Her eyes are half concealed by their extra "eyelid", the nictitating membrane that all birds can draw across to protect their delicate vision. When he has stopped, she sings her approval and he shows off a little, hopping into the air and fluttering his wings while he fans his tail. He lands on the branch, leans to his mate for a moment, and once more flutters around her, the male show-off impressing the female of his choice with his acrobatics.

Back on the perch the male once more fondles his mate, but suddenly he begins calling furiously and streaks for the bridge. Instantly the female follows, adding her voice to that of her mate. The two birds hurl themselves at an intruder, a large gray bird with a black cap that has just come by and has dared to rest awhile on the bridge. The gray jay is taken by surprise and has only time enough to flap upwards and away, letting out one indignant squeak as the phoebes run him out of their territory. Big as he is, the whisky-jack wants no part of these two belligerent bantams, who will attack even crow or raven or owl if the big birds come near their range.

When the jay has gone, the phoebes inspect their nest and soon they are busy rebuilding it, first clearing out last year's

that the bird could hear no movement within the tree in response to its preliminary tapping.

Some years ago, in another cabin that I had built in the wilderness, I was puzzled when a woodpecker repeatedly tapped on the outside of the wall within inches from my bedhead. After several early morning rousings, I inspected the plywood thoroughly but could find no trace of insects. Then I noticed my alarm clock on the orange crate that did duty as a bedside table. Its location inside the cabin corresponded exactly to the area outside where the woodpecker was hammering. I moved the ticking clock to the middle of the cabin. The woodpecker never hammered on my wall again!

Wherever there are trees, there you will find one or more of the 175 species of woodpecker that inhabit the world. In the United States and Canada twenty-two species are known, though this number may have now been reduced by one, the ivory-billed woodpecker, which appears to be extinct. This great crow-sized, black and white bird, very similar to the pileated woodpecker but with a white bill and great white wing-tips, once lived in the virgin forests of Florida and Texas, and from Illinois to South Carolina. Destruction of its habitat reduced the bird's numbers to a point of near-extinction by the mid-1930s, and today most naturalists feel that the last of these beautiful birds has passed into oblivion.

Eastern phoebe

debris, then making trips to the edge of the creek where there is a good supply of mud. A beakful at a time, the two birds ferry their "cement" and pack it in where it is needed, adding bits of twig and shreds of grass to hold it in place.

In between nest-building activities, they feed, having no trouble catching whatever insect flies through their domain, for these flycatchers are masters of the art. Twisting, dodging or dropping, no insect gets away once a flycatcher has decided to eat it. At one point, the male catches a large dragonfly, a giant of its kind almost three inches long. Back to his perch goes the phoebe and soon the dragonfly is softened up and devoured by the bird.

So they live, eating, hatching their eggs and fighting off trespassers. Twice a crow tries to raid the nest, to pick off the just-hatched young, but each time the parent birds attack the marauder and drive it off, fierce little fighters flying circles around the cumbersome robber.

At last the four young birds are raised. They fly about the

home range and soon learn to catch insects on the wing. The family has little to do but eat during the waning summer, packing on fat for their trip to the south, while filling the wilderness with their little song: *fee-be . . . fee-be . . . fe-bee . . . chip!*

The flycatcher family, to which the phoebes belong, has been aptly named Tyrannidae, "the tyrants", not because they pester other species, but because they are, as a whole, particularly belligerent in defense of their territory and are very able to cope with intruders. Swift and agile and equipped with an efficient beak, all thirty-two species of this family that live in North America will readily do battle with birds and mammals many times larger than themselves.

Because many of the family are similar in size and color, they pose problems in identification for amateur bird watchers. Most are rather large-headed, dull-colored birds with lighter underparts, that sit upright on some exposed perch, darting out now and then to snap up a passing insect in mid-air and returning to the same branch to resume their watchful pose. The beak is always lance-shaped and fringed at the base with bristle-like feathers that aid in catching insects on the wing. And all flycatchers are belligerent in nature.

The kingbirds, for instance, will unhesitatingly attack crows any chance they get. This may be because of the big black birds' nest-raiding habits, though a kingbird will chase a crow at any time, in or out of the breeding season.

The flycatcher family is also noisy! The crested flycatcher of the eastern woodlands cries loudly, *wheeeep!,* with a rising inflection. The olive-sided flycatcher yells *quick—three beers!* with abandon, from his perch on a dead tree in a northern bog or swampland. On our woodland rambles, even on the hottest summer afternoon, we hear the eastern wood pewee continually announce his name in a lazy, plaintive tone. And the eastern kingbird utters a jumble of tinkling notes on the wing, when he leaves his fence-post perch by the roadside.

And there are exceptions to the "small brown bird with a gray breast" description that fits so many of the family. The kingbird is quite striking—black above and white below, with a white band on the end of his tail that identifies him as he flies. Handsome, too, is the crested flycatcher with his brown back, rufous tail, white throat and chest, and yellow belly. Both of these species are large as flycatchers go—about eight or nine inches long.

By far the most spectacular members of the family are found in the southern United States. The scissor-tailed flycatcher is pale pearly gray with orangy-pink on its sides and beneath its wings, and about half of its twelve-to-fifteen-inch length is composed of a streaming, deeply-forked tail. This beautiful bird breeds in the region between the Mississippi and the western mountains, from southern Nebraska to Texas. The vermilion flycatcher is a resident of the Gulf Coast from Texas to Florida. The male is brilliant red below and on its head, with a black tail and back.

As a group, flycatchers are important because of their appetite for insects. Whether the birds take up residence in forest, field or town, you may be sure that their arrival signals the start of an unending war on the bugs, whether these be mosquitoes, blackflies, may beetles or cabbage butterflies.

Tousle-Head

The Frenchman River snakes its way out of the Cypress Hills in Saskatchewan, crosses the American border into Montana, and empties into the Milk River at a point just north of Interstate Highway Two. To the west, and just south of the junction of the two rivers, lies the town of Malta; to the east is the town of Glasgow, and further south the Army Corps of Engineers built the sprawling Fort Peck Reservoir. Anyone who looks at a map of this border country will quickly see that he is in the historic West, the region through which the Sioux Indians fled after the Little Big Horn battle, pursued by the United States Cavalry. This is a region of flatlands, crisscrossed by rivers and streams and occasionally interrupted by badlands, with their sudden clefts and rolling balls of tumbleweed.

A clear, fresh creek courses untidily into the Frenchman River three or four miles above its union with the Milk. A few clumps of cottonwoods stand tall beside the willows that line the creek banks, and the green of the leaves offers sudden contrast with the brownish wild grasses that grow like coarse wool on the sun-baked plains.

Sitting still and intent on a branch of a tree that overhangs the water, a large tousle-headed bird is watching the creek. He is a chunky bird some fourteen inches long, with short, almost stumpy legs, a blue-gray head and back, a white collar, and a blue-gray band across his clean white underparts. His soggy, semi-erect crest atop a head that seems too large for

A family of young kingfishers

his body gives him a roguish look, as though life is just a game, a round of sport and enjoyment. And well it may be for the male kingfisher at this time of year; the small fish are plentiful in the waters around his country, and he has already breakfasted.

As though to signify his pleasure with the state of things, he flutters off his perch in a random, darting flight and cuts loose with his harsh call. The sound is grating, like some metal ratchet slipping through a cog; it breaks the stillness of the morning as the bird swoops a circle around the creek, crossing the wider river. He swings back and settles once more on his perch, cocking one large, black eye at the clean water below.

Suddenly he launches himself anew, beak gaping as he dives at the water, his target a three-inch fish that is swimming upstream. Down knifes the fisher bird, straight into the water, with a splash and a swirl of blue and white feathers. The questing beak snaps shut, and almost in the same moment the kingfisher arches upwards, bursts out of the water and flies back to his perch, the squirming prize securely held between the long, heavy mandibles. Pause once, bang the fish against the branch, kill it, flip it into the air and grab it by the head. A gulp and a swallow and it is done; the kingfisher is ready to snooze for a while.

Up-creek, his mate is baby-sitting her brood. She resembles the male, but also has a rusty color on her sides and across her breast. Seven young kingfishers are darting and swooping up and down a stretch of water. Their efforts at fishing are clumsy, their misses frequent, as their wriggling prey swim frantically to avoid the clacking bills. The female bird has herself fed well, but she still fusses over her young ones, despite their growing ability to take care of themselves. Unlike her mate, who now prefers the quiet solitude of his own favored fishing site, she still feels some of the responsibilities of parenthood, so she remains close to her brood.

The young birds were born in a bank nest half a mile upstream. Here, both adult birds had dug a tunnel seven feet long, using their sharp beaks as pick-axes, and had fashioned at the end a round chamber. In this, on the bare earth, the female had laid eight white eggs and spent most of the next twenty-four days sitting on them. Only occasionally did the male take his turn.

Seven of the eggs hatched; the eighth was addled and was soon broken, but the adult birds did not seem to mind the stench of rotten egg which permeated the tunnel and chamber for more than a week. The blind and naked youngsters clung together in a living ball of ugliness, seeking each other's warmth, for their parents' short legs would not allow them to cover the chicks. As if to make up for this shortcoming, both male and female kingfishers busily ferried supplies to their scrawny babies, stuffing them with fish, crayfish, beetles, and even, once, a frog. In two weeks the young birds were covered in pin feathers, and a month after their birth they crawled out of the tunnel and tried out their wings for the first time.

At first, both adults spent some time training their young. The male tried first, diving on a fingerling, killing it and then dropping it on the water, where it began to float away. One youngster dived awkwardly, missed, and came up soaking wet. Another flew at the prize; he missed also. The third was rewarded and he flapped up to a tree to eat his prize. Now the mother bird dropped a dead fish and another of the young ones retrieved it. Soon all the young had been shown how to fish. From then on, they were on their own, despite their frequent attempts to coax food from their parents.

Today they were fast becoming experts, and soon they would go their own ways, as they explored farther and farther afield in their home territory. By fall they would be proficient fisher birds, healthy and sleek, well larded for their migration flight to the south.

On his perch in the cottonwood, the male kingfisher opens his eyes and holds his head to one side, as the call of his own kind intrudes upon his siesta. He looks belligerent as the harsh sound comes closer. A stranger is coming into his terri-

tory and this he will not tolerate, having staked his fishing rights to this area. The kingfisher dives off his perch and calls loudly, repeating his metallic clangor several times as he gains height in an effort to locate the intruder.

The stranger is flying in low, from the south, and the angry bird wheels to face the challenger. The two continue on a collision course and it seems as though they must crash head-on, but the stranger now notices the rightful owner of these waters. He has no wish to force an encounter, well knowing the fierceness displayed by all of his kind in the protection of their domain. He has wandered farther than usual from his own territory and was unaware of the presence of this family at the juncture of the creek. So the newcomer alters course, heading east at a sharp angle. Although the other kingfisher pursues him for a time, he gives up once the escaping bird crosses the Frenchman River.

Yelling his rusty battle cry, the kingfisher returns to his cottonwood, but not to doze this time, for the chase and the excitement have given him a new appetite. He scans the water and soon sees a small school of fish. Down he goes, gaping and straining, and once more emerges dripping from the water with a fish gripped triumphantly in his beak. Back to the tree, again to kill the fish with a quick bang against a branch, before it is swallowed.

This scene in Montana could just as easily be witnessed almost anywhere across Canada or the United States. Near lakes and streams, and beside the sea, belted kingfishers breed and sleep and catch their underwater prey, retreating in fall from the northern boundaries of their range to winter in more comfort in the southlands, while their smaller cousins, the green, or Texas kingfishers, pursue their own shrill lives in the southern parts of Arizona, New Mexico and Texas.

Belted kingfisher, male

Harbinger of Spring

The garter snake was exactly twenty-three inches long and about as thick around as my index finger, though I didn't get a chance to measure it until later. It scurried past me through the grass, where I stood watching a brown thrasher that was perched in a nearby tree. I noticed the harmless snake and I wondered why it seemed to be undertaking a purposeful journey rather than weaving along in the usual leisurely fashion of its kind. But because I was engrossed in the antics of the thrasher, which was strutting through the tree's branches emitting a variety of mimic calls, I paid but scant attention to the snake. Then the thrasher flew off, chattering, and vanished into the deep shelter of a clump of cedars growing nearby.

I lost the bird and at once my mind returned to the snake. I remembered the reptile's determined movement and I was intrigued by it, recalling that I had not hitherto noticed such determined movement by one of its kind.

How do you find a snake after it has passed you? This was a question I had never asked myself until then. But because there is always a first time for everything, I discovered that I was suddenly committed to the tracking of a snake, a task that until that moment would have elicited incredulity from me had I been offered such a challenge. After all, one can track mammals—and even birds, at times—by the imprint of their feet on the ground, but to attempt to trace the amor-

phous slitherings of a snake through long grass seemed an impossible task.

Perhaps it was the very difficulty of the thing that determined me to undertake it. It was an idle day and I was indulging myself, putting aside all thoughts of duty or accomplishment. A day of luxury, in which to dare to do nothing but watch and listen and feel and allow the elements to mold my thoughts; I still allow myself such days!

At any rate, I remained standing where I had last been when the snake slid past me, not wanting to move my feet in case I unwittingly obliterated "snake tracks", and I turned my gaze to the ground. The grass was thick, though liberally laced with weeds: chicory, Queen Anne's lace, crab grass, their leathery stems mingled with the timothy and red-top that some pioneer farmer had planted in years gone by. But there was a trail, a snake trail, indistinct to me at first because I was not used to seeking such things, but quite definite once I bent down and really studied the carpet of green that lay beneath my feet. It led relatively straight towards a tumble-down old building that had once done duty as a hen house. I followed slowly, stooped almost double, never allowing my gaze to leave the somewhat undulating trail in case I should be unable to find it again.

In a few minutes I had covered about fifteen yards and the trail was becoming quite obvious as my eyes became accustomed to its outline. Then I heard a soft rustling that was followed by a quick threshing sound and the sharp call of a bird. As I moved towards the source of these sounds, a pair of robins flew out of a cedar tree and gave vent to loud cries of alarm. I was tempted to switch my attention to these birds, but the noise ahead of me was too demanding. I had set out to track a snake and the commotion suggested that I had almost fulfilled my purpose. I took two more steps forward.

At one and the same time I tracked down the snake and discovered why the two robins had become so agitated. As I bent down to investigate the movement that had attracted my attention, I saw the garter snake tightly coiled around the struggling body of a fledgling robin, obviously an offspring of the two adult birds that were scolding excitedly and dashing from branch to branch in the nearby tree.

If I had not unwound the snake from the robin, there is no doubt the bird would have been killed, but I do not believe the reptile could have swallowed it. Despite a snake's elastic jaws, this victim was surely too large for a twenty-three-inch snake. I believe that the hunter's instinct had blindly impelled the snake to attack an animal it had little hope of swallowing whole—and whole is the only way it swallows anything.

After I released the bird and placed it on the branch of a tree, I measured the snake, let it go also, and returned my attention to the robin. It was somewhat stunned by its experience, but it recovered quickly, calling to its parents. The adults fussed and called, fluttering in and out of the small tree for some moments, then one of the birds flew off and returned in a surprisingly short time with a large earthworm. The young bird gaped and the bird stuffed the offering down its throat. Half an hour later the young robin had made the short flight from the tree to the roof of the old building and the adults returned every once in a while to feed it. As far as I am aware it recovered from its experience.

Perhaps because they represent spring in the minds of most of us who live in North America, robins are probably the most admired and best known of all our songbirds. They breed right across the continent from the tree line to southern Mexico and the Gulf States. In winter they move southward as far as Guatemala and are seldom seen north of the Canadian border.

Robins are members of the thrush family, which in North America includes eighteen species that are, to my mind, the most melodious songsters of all. Their flutelike songs ring through the woods and fields, combining with the voices of other birds to offer unforgettable moments of pleasure. Some of the family, notably the robin, are almost brazen in their habits, flying, perching, hunting and singing in the open for all to see. Others are shy birds, like the wood thrush, which prefers the shady quiet of the forest and sings continually from some hidden place.

Male robins in spring, during the mating season, can be quite fierce. The cocks migrate northward earlier than the females and lose little time in staking out a territory for themselves, though they are still tolerant of other males that may wander through their domain. But as soon as the hens arrive a few days later, the cock robin becomes jealous of his range and will furiously attack an interloping male as soon as he sees one. Sitting on some high perch that affords a clear view of the surrounding countryside, the robin sings his courting aria tirelessly, a melody that is both a love song and a battle hymn, warning other males that this is now forbidden territory.

Once, recently, while I was lounging in the spring sunshine, I was startled by the swoop of a male robin, who had been sitting in a tree watching me while he sang loudly. Suddenly the bird hurled himself from his perch and flew straight for my head, turning away only when I ducked instinctively. He landed on another tree and renewed his singing and I settled once more to watch. Again he flew at me, this time actually hitting my cap. It was then that I remembered that my headpiece was robin-breast orange. The bird took my hat for a rival! After he had flown at me for the third time, I took off the cap and propped it in a small pin cherry tree, then stepped away to watch. Almost at once the robin flew at the cap and began to peck it and claw at it, twittering furiously at the same time, and the "battle" only ended when the cap fell to the ground and landed upside down, showing the white lining. The attacker, evidently believing that he had routed his rival, returned to his first perch and began to sing. Presently he was joined by his hen, similar to him in appearance, but paler. I left them to it, but returned four weeks later to find them busy raising their brood of four in the nest that the female had built using grass cemented together with mud. During one of their many trips for insects to feed their brood, I photographed the nestlings.

I am always amazed at the robin's dexterity in worm gathering. The bird has worked out a system that amounts almost

Robin feeding young

to a science, which on many an occasion I have envied as I quartered some patch of lawn, searching in vain for a few juicy worms to use as bait for a fishing expedition. A robin will hop onto the grass and make quick little runs in various directions, standing still for a few moments at the end of each run, head tilted alertly to one side, and suddenly, peck! Lifting its head, the bird pulls and stretches a fat worm, sometimes heaving so hard it actually seems to rock back on its heels before the worm pops out like a string of glistening, brownish-pink spaghetti. How does the robin find his worm? Certainly he looks, for his quick eyes are forever scanning the ground, but some observers, myself among them, believe that the bird actually can hear the worms also, as they move underground.

To my mind, this is not too surprising when one realizes that the hearing of almost all wild animals, particularly birds, is very much more acute than our own. One might remember, further, that earthworms have on their cylindrical bodies a series of stiff, bristle-like hairs, practically invisible to the naked eye. The worm moves by expanding and contracting its body, rather like an elastic band that is pulled out and allowed to go back into its original shape again. The bristles on the worm's body anchor its forward part to the sides of its burrow while the tail end contracts forward; the rear part then braces itself with its bristles in readiness for the front part to push ahead and continue the advance. These bristles must make some kind of scraping noise as the worm moves. It is this noise, I believe, that is audible to a robin.

The Friendly One

The Lake of the Woods occupies an area between Minnesota and Ontario. Today it is well known and has become the playground for a great many tourists and cottagers, but it was still relatively remote and backwoodsy when I settled there twenty years ago, taking over a log house that had been the original homestead of a Swede who hand-dressed and numbered each and every timber.

I was a tenderfoot that midwinter day when I stepped out of my battered car and trudged through four feet of snow to reach the back door of the house. I was unprepared for the cold of the region, which registered thirty-four degrees below zero. I had been in Canada for less than a year, and I had acquired little knowledge of the country, so that I had based most of my calculations on the weather and geography of the city of Toronto. As a result, when I arrived by car to take possession of the 200 acres that I seriously intended to farm, I was dressed for the city and short boots encased my feet. Oh my, but I was cold! After spending an hour inspecting my new property I could stand no more of it.

The old wood stove in the living room, manufactured in 1889 in Minnesota, and designed for a saloon judging by the foot-ring that surrounded its pot belly, was still in good shape, but there was no wood and the chimney was in need of cleaning. I had no saw or other equipment to enable me to cut and gather firewood, so I drove to the hamlet of Bergland and there got myself fitted out for the bush country in winter. Back I went. It was mid-afternoon by the time I arrived and I was fortunate in finding a number of deadfall

trees near the house from which I cut and hauled back some branches.

By the time I had dry tamarack roaring in the stove and had thawed my sandwiches—frozen stiff by then—I felt better, but worried about the amount of wood I had on hand. There was still enough light to work by, so I went into the woods again and began cutting more fuel. I had brought the remnants of my sandwiches with me, for a snack, and had put the package on a stump.

Presently I heard a bird call, very near. I looked up. Sitting in the branch of a spruce was a gray bird, a little larger than a robin, that sported a black cap set jauntily on the back of its white head, whiskers at the base of its beak and a friendly and expectant expression in its inquisitive black eyes. Of course I had no idea what it was called, but it was a friend, alone as I was then, so I stopped working, walked over to my sandwiches and tossed a piece of bread in the general direction of the bird. I hardly expected it to stay, believing that my sudden movements would make it take flight. But not at all. The gray jay (as I later discovered it to be) hopped down onto the snow, devoured the bread and hopped closer to me, obviously asking for more. I chuckled and was happy with my new friendship and threw another piece, at the same time christening him "Oliver Twist"!

That jay stayed with me until it was too late to cut any more wood. He ate all of my food, or flew away to hide it in some cranny in a tree or rock, and before I left for the cabin he was taking food from my hand. Though I did not know then just how friendly and daring this northern species can be, I quickly realized that this fellow, at least, was different from any other bird that I had ever encountered. (It must be borne in mind that I knew little about birds or about nature in general in those days.)

Yet I feel that my future was shaped by that one jay! I felt, for the first time in my life, an instant relationship with a wild thing, a sense of friendship and companionship that was as new as it was heartwarming.

The gray jay is a hardy bird.

The next day—and every day thereafter while the cold last-
ed—I was back cutting firewood and Oliver Twist came to
keep me company and to share my sandwiches. Soon we had
worked out a routine. I would reach the logging site at eight
o'clock, cut and stack wood for two hours, then break for hot
coffee and a sandwich. The moment I tended the open fire
and hunkered down to make coffee, Oliver would fly down
and perch two or three feet from me, whistling and cooing
his impatience until I unwrapped the food and shared it with
him. By now he would often perch on my knee and take
bites as I was lifting the food to my mouth, now and then
breaking off a bigger chunk than usual and rushing off into
the bush to hide it, a compulsive habit shared by all species
of jay.

Within a week three jays attended my morning, lunch and
afternoon breaks, all equally friendly and inquisitive and
trusting. But Oliver Twist remained my favorite, a friend
whom I instinctively knew, despite the identical appearance of
all three birds.

In years to come I was to become intimately acquainted
with the gray jays of the north, spending many hours studying them and, if the truth be told, resenting the undeserved
reputation that overly-imaginative travelers have bestowed
upon them.

Certainly the gray jay, or Canada jay, is daring and even
cheeky and is ever ready to accept a handout from man. Certainly he has an uncanny sense of timing, knowing just when
food is being prepared or eaten. And certainly he will quickly
lose all fear and hop or fly right up to anybody willing to
share with him. But he is no camp robber and he does not
"carry away anything he can find", as one respected journal
says. Never have I known a whisky-jack "seize bacon right
out of the frying pan", as one book claims. To start with, the
gray jay is highly intelligent and will not expose its delicate
feathers to the heat of a fire or be stupid enough to burn its
mouth with hot bacon. I do not doubt that if someone left a
panful of food away from the fire and was not there to take

Gray jay, Canada jay, or whisky-jack

care of it, a jay would quickly believe the pan and its contents was an offering, but I will not accept that the bird actually steals right from under the noses of campers.

Gray jays, admittedly, are mischievous and will take any food they can find. Sometimes they may pick up some inedible object in the belief that it will turn out to be digestible, but the birds are not, in my opinion, the pests that some "authorities" make them out to be.

Gray jays are hardy creatures and more prone than most other birds to store food for later consumption. Living for many months of the year at subzero temperatures and raising their young when the snow is still on the ground, these birds must feed continuously in order to stay alive.

Deep inside the shelter of a branchy evergreen, often as early as February, the jays construct a substantial cup of twigs, leaves, grass and mosses, lined with hair, feathers and fine grasses. The rim of the nest fits closely to the female's body, trapping her heat and in this way maintaining the correct incubating temperature in spite of the cold weather. Usually three or four eggs are laid, though five is not unusual, and the chicks hatch after about eighteen days of incubation by the female.

At times, the gray jay will whistle shrilly, not unlike a red-shouldered hawk; on other occasions it may squeak, chirp and coo softly. But, when the mood strikes it, it can sing quite well, emitting a long, soft, flutelike song. The fluffy gray plumage and black cap, the absence of a crest, its large size and the northwoods habitat in which it lives, make the gray jay an easy bird to recognize, as well as an attractive companion in the northern wilderness.

Voice of the Northland

Under a canopy of blazing stars and highlighted by the silver of a full moon, the rock-bordered lake looks tranquil and even a little lonely this night in the northern wilderness. The water and the land that surrounds it have been here for countless ages, nameless and unknown to all but a very few men.

The lake is seven miles long and two miles across at its widest point and it lies pointing north and south, obtaining its cold, clear waters from three fair-sized streams that empty into it at its northeast shore. At its southernmost point a fourth stream releases spill-off water in times of heavy rain and is also fed year-round by an unseen spring on the lake bottom. The lake and the land are unspoiled, too remote for the inroads of a demanding civilization, and thus secure. The forest holds stands of spruce and birch and poplar. In some places the stands are pure spruce, in others the silver of birch and the green-white of poplar mix with the more somber colors of the conifers.

The lake is the heart of this land, keeping it green with its moisture, giving sanctuary to many of the animals and birds of the region and offering water to those that are thirsty. It is a stopping place for timber wolves and deer and moose; it is home each summer to ducks and geese and loons.

Tonight, under the bright moon, the loons are frisking. The breeding season is over. This is late summer and the cares of nesting and rearing the young birds are over. Now old and young roam at will, dashing back and forth atop the water with much splashing of the big webbed feet, diving in

pursuit of bass and pickerel. Just now they are silent, though their actions are almost as boisterous as their voices.

Half a mile away, sitting or lying in the shelter of a thick stand of spruce, relaxed upon the deep carpet of moss underfoot, seven timber wolves are taking their ease after a good hunt. The old pair have led the pups well and the young wolves have learned their lessons, so that the kill came quickly and the pack members filled their bellies. Now they are idle in the way that wild things have, a tranquil and contented laziness that is shared by all and savored fully. The big dog, the father, a battle-scarred veteran of many hunts, lies flat on his side, tongue lolling out with his panting, now and then twitching some part of his hide as a persistent mosquito sucks out a little blood. The bitch, the mother wolf, sits. She, too, lets her tongue hang loose, breathing deeply and in this way sweating, cooling her body by the evaporation of moisture. The pups are still licking their chops and their paws and those hard-to-reach places on the chest, where some of the deer's blood adheres, still fresh and red.

Presently the male wolf sits up, yawns, licks his lips once and howls. The long, deep wail rises into the night and hangs over the forest. Instantly the others join and the seven voices chorus the song of the wolf pack.

The loons listen, and are still for a short time; then the deep ululations coming from the forest strike some responsive chord. The birds begin their own wild cackle, their shrill, ribald laughter blending with the deep tones of the wolves, filling the night with a strident cacophony. The loons get more and more excited as the song progresses. They dash over the water in crazy circles, one or two at a time, sometimes all at once, and their eerie calls ring out again and again, even after the wolves have stopped their song.

Slowly the loons wind down, but single birds persist, launching their tremulous cries as they swim, plaintive and sad at one moment, gleeful and frivolous the next. A nighthawk dives, and on the upturn his stiff wings produce a strumming sound rather like the twanging of an elastic band,

---

Common loon turning her eggs

then the night flier calls in his nasal voice—*peent, peent*—fluttering before each cry. A whip-poor-will chants his name endlessly as he squats on top of a warm rock.

Suddenly there is silence, and then the sound of lapping. The timber wolves have come to drink. They stand strung out along a low point of shore, some up to their bellies in the water, others daintily stretching out their necks, not wanting to get their feet wet. For a time the animals and birds of the lake respect the presence of the wolves, then a loon disdains the hunters, knowing that it is quite safe. The bird calls again, his voice quivering, sounding impatient. The others respond and soon the whole lake echoes with the wild halloos. This is too much for the wolves. One by one they turn and lope along the trail, back to their spruce sanctuary and to sleep. The lake belongs again to the birds and they splash and play as before, their voices filling the silver night.

Four pairs of loons dropped into the lake last spring from their wintering grounds off the Florida coast, mated and produced six young birds in total. Each pair selected its own particular area and built a simple nest among the reeds and rushes, respecting the territory of the others and guarding its home ground fiercely.

Common loons they were, a name that seems demeaning for such handsome creatures, each bird dark-headed, ruby of eye, with a sleek white collar striped finely with black, the body pebbled white and black with a snowy chest, the beak long and strong and pointed. Common loons! What a name for the great feathered divers that can kick down under water in pursuit of fish and are so strong and graceful in flight, though cumbersome on land because of their short legs.

Common loons, they are called, nevertheless, to distinguish them from other North American members of the family Gaviidae: the red-throated loon with red flash on gray throat, zebra-striped nape and plain dark body, smaller than the "common" but a loon in manner born and just as able to fling its loud voice at the wilderness; the Arctic loon, a fawn-headed bird with black bib, white chest and checkered white

Common loon

Arctic loon

patches on its sooty wings and back; and the big, three-foot-long yellow-bill, head shining with green and purple hues, and with light-colored, upturned bill. These three species nest usually farther north than the widespread common loon, in the Northwest Territories and the arctic islands. The red-throated loon winters along the Atlantic and Pacific coasts from the Arctic to Mexico, the arctic loon down the Pacific coast from Alaska to lower California, and the yellow-billed loon in southeastern Alaska. The common loon may be seen on both east and west coasts in winter, and occasionally on the Great Lakes.

These are true birds of the northland, big, handsome and never forgotten by those who hear their calls.

Birds of the Nahanni

The Nahanni River gouges its way through the Northwest Territories of Canada, swift and cold, to the point where it drops spectacularly at Virginia Falls, a cascade that dwarfs the plunge of Niagara. The Nahanni is inaccessible and mysterious, a place of ancestral ghosts and unspoiled loveliness.

Here came two miners, made a strike and parted. One came out, to claim that his partner had disappeared. Searchers went in and found the missing man, decapitated. The secret of his death remains. Came another man. He, too, died and was found headless. No one knows why.

It has a character all its own, this wild river, and it touches the human who ventures into its domain; is it the spirit of the waters, or the ghosts of long ago still wandering lost in this magnificent region? Who knows! But the river casts a spell on the man who goes to it. And it speaks, summer and winter it speaks, its voice a constant liquid sound, at times a soft murmur, at other times a great and fearsome roar as its waters boil and froth and shoot spray high into the air.

There is a place near Virginia Falls where two massive blocks of granite tower upwards for more than thirty feet, square, craggy monoliths that could have come from some ancient giant's sculpting tools. At the foot of these monsters there is an overhang that offers shelter, a cave-like hollow facing south and thus protected from the winds that even in summer have the power to bite as they slip down the icy faces of the surrounding mountains.

The month is September. It brings frost at night, sharp winds, the deep baying of the timber wolves. Ice crusts over open pools each morning and most of the birds are ready to leave, for the Nahanni is not hospitable in winter.

Atop the tallest of the two granite statues grows a gnarled and twisted evergreen. It has hung on there, precariously, for many years and should, by now, have added girth to its trunk and length to its branches. But growth has been very slow in that exposed position. The tree is stunted and twisted and thin and will remain thus until age and the elements destroy it. Perched on one of the corkscrew limbs of the tree sits a great black bird, unruffled by the bite of wind, or by the loneliness, or by the spirit of the river that groans noisily as it slithers along its causeway.

The raven fluffs his shiny black feathers and stares into space. Maybe he is thinking about the fast-approaching winter that will plunge temperatures down to forty and fifty degrees below zero and dump crystalline snow in deep drifts that will blow like white powder, reaching even the tree in which he now sits. Or perhaps he is just drowsy.

In the sky to the south, high up, appears a black dot. It looks like a punctuation mark on a blank page. The hunched raven notes it, is aware of its movement. He opens his beak and calls once, harshly. He watches the dot. Soon the punctuation mark becomes a black dash; then it takes on new shape. Now the wings of a bird are clear and again the raven croaks, this time calling twice. The approaching bird answers with another croak and soon they are talking as the newcomer descends and prepares to land in the twisted tree.

Moments after its arrival the second bird sits fluffed out beside the first and both ravens are quiet and contemplative. They are young, this year's brood, so perhaps they wonder what this new barren time is going to bring, for this is their home and here they will stay to face whatever the winter has in store for them.

As though at some silent signal, both birds suddenly leap from their perch and fly to the foot of the granite block. The remnants of a campsite are there, fresh, for the man who spent a month beside the river has only recently gone to the outside, to the shelter of civilization. The ravens must inspect this place; they must poke at the ashes of the dead campfire and hunt through the rocky alcove, for there may be something edible left around the camp.

While one bird rummages by the fireplace, the second bird enters the dimly-lit cave and searches it industriously. The quick black eyes miss nothing. Held in a crack between two rocks the raven sees a strip of dull silver. He walks to it and pulls out a piece of dry skin that was peeled away from a fat trout more than two weeks earlier. Quickly the raven scuttles away with it to the darkest corner of the cave, jealous of his find and swallowing hastily, before his companion notices. But the other bird herself has made a find, a small mound of bacon fat adhering to a flat rock beside the fireplace. She quickly pecks at the savory, as anxious as the male bird to eat it all before she is discovered.

When these snacks are eaten, the hen leaves the ring of rocks that formed the fireplace and enters the cave, while the male leaves the cave and begins to search the ashes, each bird hopeful that the other has missed something. But there is nothing more now; only the blackened ring of rocks and the little pile of ashes testify to the visit of man. As the ravens strut about they chatter to each other, alternating the hoarse croaks with a few buzzing notes and clipped, gulping sounds. At last they are satisfied that nothing edible has been overlooked and the male flaps clumsily off the ground, followed by the female. The two have not mated yet, but they have become paired and will probably remain together all winter and mate next spring—if both survive.

Now they fly over the Nahanni, high up, planing on level wings almost like eagles and scanning the ground below in search of carrion or some small and incautious animal. The land over which they fly is immense and majestic and their eyes miss not a single detail of it: the crags, the densely-packed evergreens, the occasional open space. Suddenly the male raven, a little ahead of the female, veers sharply towards the north. The hen bird turns also and quickly notes that which has attracted her partner's attention. More than 1,000 feet below the two birds, and at least a mile to the north, a pack of wolves has made a kill and is now feeding on the carcass of an aging bull moose.

There will be a feast left for the two birds and they hurry to the scene, anxious lest other ravens discover it. In a short time they flap down and settle in a tree close to the feeding wolves. Two of the predators glance upwards, but quickly return to the eating, ignoring the black birds. The ravens wait, but the sight of so much meat and the gnawing of their own hunger makes them impatient and they strut up and down their perch, croaking, as though urging the wolves to hurry. Still the pack ignores them and the male bird cannot contain himself any longer.

Down he flaps to land some ten feet from the wolves, which continue eating. The raven moves closer and sees a few scraps of meat and sinew lying a little distance from the circle of wolves; these were left there, no doubt, after some part of the carcass had been dragged aside. The raven risks a

Common raven

quick grab. Moving forward with his strange, stilted gait, the big bird pecks at a piece of meat, nips it with his beak, and quickly jumps into the air and flaps away. Only one wolf deigns to take notice.

Seeing this, the female bird also drops to the ground and hops over to the remaining bits of meat. She, too, is rewarded with a meal and is allowed to fly off to eat it. The wolves are almost sated, and so long as the daring birds do not actually alight on the carcass they will not molest the ravens. Young as they are, the big birds seem to be aware of this. Still, it takes nerve to come so close to nine northern wolves. And nerve the ravens certainly do have!

Nerve, endurance, a highly-developed intelligence and the keenest eyes in the business are raven characteristics, their stock in trade that allows them to survive in seemingly impossible places under conditions that would be intolerable to any other bird.

When these two were yet hatchlings, they watched as their parents routed an attacking gyrfalcon, a deadly, fierce predator to most, but no match for the ravens, who outflew it and almost killed it with their heavy, sharp beaks. Another time they saw three ravens force a golden eagle to drop an arctic hare it was carrying in one taloned foot.

The two were born in a big, bulky nest made of sticks and lined with a variety of soft materials such as moss and discarded feathers. As they grew, their natural curiosity drew them to the edge of the nest, to watch the doings of the adult birds, and to observe the world of the Nahanni beneath their nesting tree. The young ravens became more and more daring until one morning, first one then another chick dived into space and flapped its newly-feathered wings. Four young ravens acquired skill of flight that day, and soon they became able to hunt for themselves, to steal from others, and to spot carrion as they flew over their wild world. They also learned to work together, at times a pair of them hunting as a team, one bird distracting the attention of lemming or ground squirrel while the other attacked swiftly from behind.

And now they were stout and strong and bold, and ready to face their greatest test—winter in the land of the Nahanni.

The Bold One

Upon hearing the raucous chatter of a flock of blue jays, the average listener is tempted to conclude that these bright blue birds with their grayish underparts are poor songsters, endowed with misdirected enthusiasm for the sound of their own voices. Yet the blue jay can sing, softly and cooingly, when it has a mind to.

Hearing a pair of these bustling, active birds during the courting season, one would not believe, unless one actually saw them doing it, that the soft, lovey-dovey sounds were made by the usually brash and shrill coxcombs. In addition, blue jays, like all their family, are great mimics and love to copy the calls of other birds, particularly the two-syllabled whistle of the hunting red-shouldered hawk. I have seen a jay pipe like a chickadee, trill like a blackbird and caw like a crow. In between times, their normal repertoire of shrieks and screams fills the woods with sounds reminiscent of the jungle.

The blue jay is one of the most widespread and easily recognized birds east of the Rockies. It is as much at home in the city as in the forest and is ever ready to take seeds or other foodstuffs from the bird feeder. It is active and daring, yet cautious, quick to duck into the shelter of tree or shrub at the slightest alarm, but just as ready to make a dash to get some morsel of food if it thinks it has the slightest chance of getting away with it.

Probably the majority of blue jays migrate somewhat southward during the fall, spending the cold months as far down

Blue jay

Feeding a hungry brood

as the Gulf States, but many stay in the north, enduring below-zero temperatures and seeming to be none the worse for the hard winter when the spring flocks return prior to mating.

At this time they are boisterous and noisy, full of the joys of the new season, dashing busily from tree to clearing to bush and clowning exuberantly, their repeated cries resounding through the forest: *jay! jay! jay!*

When the courting season arrives, the birds pair off and become quite subdued, electing to disappear into the shrubbery where they carry on the age-old rituals, burbling and cooing softly to each other as the nesting time gets closer.

In an evergreen or deep in a brushy thicket, both birds build a platform of small sticks and twigs on which they fashion a bulky nest from shreds of bark, grass, old leaves, fur, feathers, or any other soft material they can find. In the neighborhood of man, bits of wool, paper and string are taken for the nest lining, which is often laid on a base of mud. The nest is about seven inches across and three inches deep. Inside this cup the female lays between four and six brown, bluish or greenish eggs, spotted with brown or olive, and incubates them for about seventeen days.

While the female is sitting, the male attentively feeds her, though, like many other birds, he does not rush in directly to the nest. Instead he hops quietly to the bottom of the tree and climbs it spirally, sliding his way in, probably in an attempt to keep secret the location of his family's home.

When the young hatch, both birds spend the next three weeks finding food for the voracious chicks, feeding them about every ten or twelve minutes of the day.

Like all members of the Corvid family—which includes jays, crows and magpies—the blue jay is highly intelligent, bold and gregarious. It will eat anything, including quantities of insects and carrion in addition to its staple diet of nuts, seeds, and fruit. Like its relatives, too, it is given to raiding the nests of other birds, a habit that does not endear it to some bird lovers. But these predatory tactics are better regarded as part of nature's plan to keep the small bird population in check. After all, if all the young birds of every species were to survive to maturity, the world would soon be overrun with birds and they would die from want of food. And from man's point of view, a world swarming with even the most beautiful songsters would not be a desirable place to live. Neither does the blue jay always have its own way. It must endure the attacks of the smaller birds, which harry the jay whenever it comes near their nesting sites, and usually it is forced to retreat before it can do any damage to eggs or young.

Jays are particularly fond of acorns and beechnuts and when they have crammed their stomach to the point where one more would be too much they will bury nuts in the ground for future use. Often, I am sure, they forget where some of their stores are hidden and in this way they help to seed the forest.

On occasion a jay will fall out with a red squirrel when the little redback discovers the bird's cache and proceeds to help himself to it. The jay, though stopping short of grappling with the furry robber, screams his anger continuously and makes fast, darting flights at the intruder, now and then landing a sharp peck. But the squirrel usually persists and, in his turn roundly cursing the jay, dodges swiftly each time the bird flies at him. These harmless duels may last for quite some time and even after the squirrel gives up, the outraged jay follows him through the woods, shrilling his anger and sometimes attracting other jays who join in the chase, until the squirrel, irritated beyond the point of endurance, dives into some convenient hiding place.

By the same token, the jays are always willing to raid a squirrel's food cache, at which time the distraught redback stands quivering with rage on top of his hoard, ducking each time a jay dives, and shrilling his curses at the robbers. Usually the jays win in these battles, for several will band together and, while the defending squirrel's attention is centered on one bird, another will sweep in and grab whatever it can.

Often, too, jays will steal from each other, creating pandemonium within a flock when one bird finds some particularly succulent tidbit and is immediately set upon by the rest. Then, usually, the fortunate bird dashes away into the forest, somehow managing to scream its protest even with the food in its mouth.

When they are not feeding themselves or their young, jays will roam about the forest in large flocks, as though bored and looking for mischief, and they take seeming pleasure in mobbing a would-be predator, such as an owl or a hawk, which has no choice but to flee the concerted attack of a dozen or more screaming jays.

In the mountains and west to the Pacific coast, from Alaska to Central America, the blue jay's counterpart is the Steller's jay. This is a more somber bird, but handsome nevertheless—dark blue throughout, with a blackish head and a pronounced crest. Over each eye it sometimes has a conspicuous white, slightly curved flash, rather like an arched eyebrow. It looks too much like its eastern cousin to be taken for anything but a jay and it has the same noisy characteristics, though it calls *shook! shook! shook!* instead of *jay! jay! jay!*

Constant Flyers

The farmhouse in which I once lived had a ramshackle old porch from which I had removed the sagging door when I took up residence. Inside this porch, on the two-by-four timbers that supported the rafters, two pairs of barn swallows built their mud nests the spring after my arrival. At first the birds would panic each time I went in or out of the house, but after a week they got used to my comings and goings and continued sitting on their brown-spotted white eggs. In due course the young swallows hatched, and that's when the trouble started.

The blue jay was large and especially fearless, daring to do what none of the other jays in the area would do: enter the porch to steal the tiny swallow chicks. The other jays were evidently deterred by my frequent presence from entering the porch. But that particular jay wasn't going to be balked by any human, and the result was that he continually raided the two nests while the parent swallows were out capturing food for their young. The results were sad. Each female had laid a maximum clutch of eggs, five, and all of them had hatched, but by the fourth day only one baby swallow was left in each nest and the adults were frantic in their efforts to stop the robber.

The jay was determined! But he never did manage to escape with even one of the baby swallows because, having grasped the less-than-two-inch hatchling, the robber was immediately attacked by the adult swallows, all four ganging up on him. In the close quarters of the porch the jay could not maneuver and as a result, after a few desperate attempts to

Barn swallow

reach the open door, he would drop the tiny bird on the board floor and fly out. Each time I would find the evidence of his thievery and, despite my liking for jays, I was often tempted to put an end to that particular thief, because, of course, the nestlings were dead when I found them.

On the fifth day after the hatching, when I left the house first thing in the morning, the last two nestlings were lying dead on the porch floor. Well, that was that, I thought. At least the ordeal for the swallows—and for me—was over. But I had not reckoned on the determination of the swallows. Soon each female had laid a new clutch of eggs, four in one nest, five again in the other, and they began incubating anew, males and females sharing the task. Fifteen days later there were nine gaping little mouths belonging to nine ugly nestlings reaching for food every minute of the day, keeping the adults busy catching enough insects.

Then the jay was back. I found one of the babies dead on the third morning and again the adults were frantic. I could not, of course, stand guard over those nests right through the day and I could not put the door back on because this would also keep out the swallows, so I decided that I would take a hand in the unequal contest and shoot just that one jay. I didn't like the idea at all, but neither could I bear to keep on picking up those little cadavers from my porch floor every day.

The next day, not looking forward to my task but determined to carry it out, I rose early, long before the thief was about, opened the front door and sat myself just inside its shelter, from where I could see the porch door and get a shot at the thief with my .410 gauge shotgun. I had to catch the killer in the act, else I could not pick him out from among the several other blue jays that frequented my front yard.

By first light I had almost had enough of my vigil; the mosquitoes made much of their opportunity to feed off my person and, despite my frequent use of repellent, punctured my hide in a great many places. But each time I was tempted to quit I remembered those stiff, blue little uglies that I had been picking up off the floor, and my anger at the jay kept me at my post. Soon the adult swallows flitted out of the porch to get breakfast for their young. Now, I thought, the killer will come. But he didn't. An hour went by, then another. It was almost seven o'clock in the morning and I was itching all over from the bites. Besides, I was hungry and wanted my morning coffee. So I left my post to make coffee and grab a quick bite to eat.

No sooner had I returned and settled down, coffee mug in hand and already journeying to my lips, than a flash of blue entered the doorway and the jay made a quick dash at the nearest nest, reaching in with his heavy, sharp beak and grabbing at one baby. I tried to set down the mug and grab the gun in time to get a shot at the jay, but all I managed to do was to spill hot coffee on my thighs and drop the gun.

While I was going through these antics, two swallows swooped in and darted at the jay, who dropped the baby swallow and fled. I rose and carefully picked up the young bird. At least this one was alive! I was not at all sure that it would survive the jay's rough handling and the unceremonious fall onto the wooden floor, but I put it back in the right nest. Then I settled down, ignoring the coffee and holding the gun at the ready, to wait for the return of the jay.

Perhaps half an hour went by and I was beginning to think that my presence, which the killer bird could not have failed to notice as I moved to get the gun, had scared him away. Then two of the swallows came in with food for their young and, after they had fed the babies, headed again for the doorway.

It was at this very moment that the jay elected to come back. The results were startling to me and even more so to the jay. As he flew in at speed, the two swallows were flying out, and the three birds collided in mid-air. The swallows, being much more nimble, recovered first, continued outside, turned, and swooped back in, emitting their distress calls and drawing the other two adult swallows to the porch. The jay, in the meantime, obviously disoriented and shaken by the collision, tried to scramble out of the porch, spurred to frantic action by my own movement as I rose once more to put an end to him.

Instead of flying outside, the stunned jay flew right into my living room, made a beeline for one of the windows and hit the glass with a thump that knocked him almost senseless. He fell on the chesterfield and I thought he was dead. But when I saw him move a second or two later, I quickly closed the front door. Now I had the villain!

Before he could recover his ability to fly, I reached him and picked him up—only just in time, too, for he immediately began to struggle quite powerfully. When he found he could not get away from me, he leaned over and bit me on the thumb several times, pinching quite hard with his strong beak. I was glad he elected to bite rather than peck, for I am sure his sharp beak would have drawn blood. But I had him and I knew the swallows would now be able to raise their young.

Well, I had a number of cages which I used, as occasion demanded, to raise injured animals and birds when these came my way, so rather than kill him, I decided to imprison the thief until the swallows had managed to raise their young.

The barn swallow builds a sturdy nest of mud, lined with soft feathers

This I did, much to the jay's disgust, though he was not disgusted enough to stop eating, which he did voraciously. After a time he even got quite tame, though he would vent his spleen at me on occasion by screaming madly and attracting the notice of the other jays, who called back in chorus, so it was not too peaceful around my home for a time.

While the jay was serving his sentence I spent a lot of my spare moments watching the swallows and marveling at the enormous appetite of their young. The adults were ceaseless and untiring in their task of catching insects for the young birds and averaged a trip a minute, more or less.

I had been fascinated earlier by their nest building, noting the hundreds of trips that the birds made from mud-puddle to porch, each time carrying a little ball of mud which they put into place and tamped with their tiny beaks and then further secured by weaving in straw or old grasses. They finished by

Fledgling swallows

adding a lining of fine grass, hair and feathers.

Knowing that swallows almost invariably return to the same nesting sites, and frequently take over and rebuild last year's nests, I made myself a promise to return the porch door to its proper place before next spring, because I feared that the errant jay, if he survived the winter, might well decide to try again.

I have always had a special affection for swallows and an admiration of their sleek shapes. With wings like sabers and a streamlined body ending in a more or less forked tail, these birds are designed for almost constant flight. In fact, so specialized have they become that their short legs are almost useless for walking.

All of the twelve species of swallow that are found in North America are industrious insect eaters, feeding on the wing by gaping, that is, flying swiftly through clouds of insects with mouth wide open. They are mostly sociable birds that build their nests close together in small or large communities.

The barn swallows are dark metallic blue on the upper part of their body, have a chestnut bib and forehead and are pale cinnamon on the underside. Their tail has a deep fork and is patched with white. Before civilized man put up barns and other buildings, barn swallows used to nest on rocky cliffs and other such places where angle and an overhead shelter gave them sanctuary.

The cliff swallow, on the other hand, builds against a wall or rock face, constructing a mud nest shaped rather like a half gourd. The bank swallows, small birds with a brown back and a brown band across the white breast, dig out homes in some convenient sand bank, but the purple martin likes a frame home, using a hole in a tree or, preferably, a well-designed apartment house built by human hands.

Whatever the species and however they nest, swallows are to be encouraged around the human habitation. They are sure to pay for the little mess they make by picking off countless swarms of insects. For this reason alone, anybody who has ever been well bitten by blackflies or mosquitoes will always reserve a special place for these beautiful and charming little birds.

Champion of Speed

Standing beside her four downy young, a peregrine falcon stares intently at a high, distant speck that is moving towards the rocky cliff ledge upon which she has built her scanty nest. The young birds, two weeks old now, are screeching, demanding food.

The sky-dot comes nearer and the female peregrine watches as her mate aims his sleek shape towards the nesting site. From one of his taloned feet hangs the lifeless body of a duck, a teal drake that rose over the water while the tiercel was hunting for his family. Gliding high over the marshland, the peregrine immediately spotted the rising duck and went into his stoop, a dive powered by height and by the half-folded wings that sent him rocketing downwards at 175 miles an hour. As the tiercel closed with his quarry, the duck heard the wind humming through his stiff pinions. The teal tried to dodge, but the maneuver was useless. In seconds the falcon closed and with his clenched foot struck the duck a smashing blow on the head, splitting the skull. As the lifeless teal was about to fall back into the water, the peregrine swooped again and deftly caught the duck in his talons, rising immediately and gaining height as he sped back to the cliff nest.

Still flying high, but close to the nest now, the tiercel relaxes his talons and lets the duck drop, and as the teal's dead weight tumbles downwards the female peregrine launches herself from the ledge, flies straight up, and catches the food with ease, carrying it to her young. The male, mean-

Peregrine falcon

time, circles once over the cliff, then turns, seeking food for himself this time.

On the ledge the four chicks are frantic as the female lands with the teal. They are now able to pluck at the kills that are brought to them, and the mother falcon tears at the duck, letting the young feed, but eating of it herself also. Soon there is nothing left but some feathers and a few scraps of bloody skin and some bones. The peregrine returns to her perch, to wait for her mate again, while the young fight over the bits of food that are left, stealing from each other, first one, then another mantling some morsel, extending its unfledged wings over the food to protect it from the others.

On his way back to the marsh the male peregrine sees a crow. He launches himself in pursuit and soon the crow lies dead on the ground and the male falcon is sailing down to eat. After his meal, he will kill once more for his family and mate, and he will do it as easily and swiftly, as cleanly as before, for he is the perfect hunting bird that has no match for speed and agility in flight.

Last spring the two birds returned to their far northern nesting site after spending the winter near the Canadian border, whence they had followed the migratory birds that are their food supply. After putting on a graceful display of courting aerobatics for his mate, the tiercel helped in remodeling the nest—a simple task, for the peregrine is not an elaborate home builder. Later the female laid four buffy eggs that were heavily streaked with reddish, almost mahogany-colored lines. She brooded her eggs for thirty-four days, sitting patiently while the tiercel hunted and ferried food back to her, dropping it from on high for her to catch.

A week has passed and the female rises to join her mate. It is afternoon; the young falcons are sated and dozing and both adults have eaten their fill. The falcons frolic in the sky, swooping and diving and circling. Once a big mallard flies in low towards the water and both falcons chase it, playfully,

Peregrine perched near its nest

seeming to enjoy this game. The mallard, terrified and quacking loudly, tries to avoid them, but they easily keep up with her, pushing her this way and that. Then, as though tired of the game but wishing to score a point, the female falcon darts in close to the mallard and taps her gently with one clenched foot, and the falcons break away, leaving the startled duck to plunge protesting into the water and scurry for the shelter of the reeds.

In their dives, some of which reach speeds of almost three miles a minute, the sleek hunters are aided by a system of baffles built into their nostrils, for at such speeds they would not be able to breathe without some means of deflecting the rush of air.

By late afternoon both birds return to the nest, the female carrying a rather large sandpiper for her young. As the chicks feed, the adults perch on the rock ledge, preening and resting.

They are similar and striking in appearance, about the size of a crow, a dark ashy-blue above, with a well-defined, drooping black mustache that contrasts clearly with the white throat. Below, the birds are white, finely barred with black, and their long, pointed wings are darkish beneath, mottled with white.

In the fall, when their young are fully fledged and ready for the long flight south, the falcons will follow the streaming flocks of migratory birds to spend the winter in the United States, or even Mexico.

Gallant Gander

In autumn, the colorful pause before the winter solstice,
those of us who live in the northern part of this continent direct our thoughts towards fuel and storm windows, and most
of the birds turn their backs on the cold. For many people,
there is something about the fall that has power to stir up
memories. They feel restless, nostalgic for the things of yesterday.

It was just before duck-hunting season one year that I set
out for a walk through the wilderness of Ontario, in an area I
knew well and which was filled with the scarlet wonders of
maple. After about an hour of walking through heavy stands
of trees, I found a downed log for a seat and contemplated
a small clearing that marked the northern boundary of the
maple bush. Behind this clearing stretched an immense tract
of forest and from the knoll upon which I sat the view was
marvelous.

A mixture of evergreen and deciduous trees greeted my
eyes. Glowing leaves mingled their shades of yellow and rus-
set and red and brown with the green needles of pine and
spruce. The sun shone brightly and the sky was cloudless;
the hunting guns had not yet begun to blast. It was a perfect
autumnal day.

I had sat there for perhaps an hour, in contemplative
peace, when I heard the cry of the wild geese. I looked up
and I saw them, flying high and fast in a thin, irregular, ar-
rowhead formation, a living wedge of Canada geese that almost instantly switched my thoughts backwards in time. Still
hearing the incessant cries of the birds overhead, I remem-

bered one of their kind, a gander, who could not find it in himself to abandon his mate after she had been wounded by shotgun pellets.

The hunters had taken their toll and had left the wilderness, when I saw the big goose for the first time. It was a typical day of December in the northland: ice-filled, still, a fresh fall of snow smothering the land.

Imagine a bush trail, a thin, indistinct path beaten into the snow that is pockmarked by the hoofs of deer and moose, by the pads of timber wolves and foxes; here and there, there is sign that a bobcat has loped along the snow trail, while off the compacted surface the imprints of snowshoe hares are clear.

The trail snakes its way through the spruce and tamarack, the former green and snow laden, the latter bare of needles, for they are the only coniferous trees that shed their leaves in the fall. Underfoot, beneath the snow, lies the muskeg; peat bogland that in areas stretches for miles, land that is not quite land, but is instead a sort of liquid compost formed of the fallen leaves and branches and trees that have decomposed through the ages. In December this liquid mulch is frozen, offering good footing, but in spring there are places here that are seemingly bottomless, treacherous bog holes thinly carpeted by innocent moss. This is a wild land, densely timbered, desolate-seeming to those more accustomed to the order of town and city.

I knew the country well, for I had spent two years in it and had depended upon it for most of my daily needs. Beyond the trail I was following lay a small lake which was the home of two beaver families and the drinking place, during ice-free times, of the deer, the moose, the bear, the timber wolf and the many other animals and birds that struggled for life in that region. From spring to fall that lake was bustling with activity, but on that day in December it was silent, icebound. Yet there were signs of life: tracks of weasel and mink, of

Canada goose

otter and fox, of snowshoe hare, and here and there the clear imprints of bird wings in the snow where gray jay or chickadee had landed for some tidbit, or a hawk had swooped down upon a hapless mouse.

Emerging from the trail into the open near the lake, I stopped to inspect the white surface, wondering whether I would find much change along the shoreline since my last visit two months earlier, and I noted almost at once that the beaver had logged off the poplars on a sharp point of land that projected towards the center of the lake.

It was early morning, about eight o'clock as I recall, and the sun had not long passed above tree level, so that it was reflected from the snow surface, creating an intense glare. Because of this I thought at first that the lake's surface was deserted. Then I heard a noise, a soft, intense hissing that was accompanied now and then by a flapping sound.

Squinting against the sun, I peered more closely, my attention being drawn by the sounds to a spot near the larger of the two beaver lodges. I saw movement, but I could not yet distinguish the characters in the drama that was even then developing. I moved closer and angled away from the sun before using the field glasses I always carry with me. At last I could see clearly.

Backed up against the snow-coated sticks of the beaver lodge was a Canada goose, his long neck outstretched, his great wings open and poised ready to deliver a blow. In front of him crouched a red fox, a small vixen I judged, hungry yet cautious, wanting to kill but fearing the power of the goose's wing blows. Beside the threatened bird lay a still bundle of black and white. Another goose; it looked dead.

I suppose I should have let nature take its course, but I could not simply stand by and watch while the snowbound goose was killed by the fox, for it was clearly weakening and the outcome was inevitable.

I moved closer, my snowshoes crunching on the snow, and the fox looked up, startled. For a moment it peered at my advancing figure and, as its attention left the goose, the bird

Male and female Canada geese look alike

lashed at it with one wing, striking it a glancing blow. The fox turned and ran, quickly reaching the shoreline and disappearing into the bush.

I walked up close to the goose and he turned his fury on me. For a time I kept my distance, wondering what I should do; then I decided. Taking off my parka, I used it as a shield to muffle the still-powerful wing blows that were delivered by the goose as soon as I was in range. With the help of the coat I pinned his wings while I checked his body for injuries. There were none, but starvation and cold had combined to weaken the bird and his bones lay hard against his skin.

Nearby lay the body of the other goose, whom I judged to be his mate though it was impossible then to be sure, as among geese the sexes are identical in appearance. One of her legs was mangled by shot, one wing broken. On the other side of the dead bird was a small area of open water, little more than an eighteen-inch hole, near the beaver lodge, where the ice is always the thinnest. The goose had not been dead long, for her body was still slightly warm.

It did not take me long to piece together the incidents of the wilderness drama. Six, perhaps seven weeks earlier, when the hunting season opened, the two birds had probably been part of a flock heading south. The goose had been wounded, but her height and speed had allowed her to travel some distance before setting down on the surface of this out-of-the-way lake. Because geese often remain partners for life, the gander had broken his journey and followed his mate. Once in this place they were safe from human hunters, but the goose could travel no farther and the gander, gallant but unable to help her, had stayed with his mate.

The weeks had come and gone. The gander fought with the encroaching ice, trying to maintain a reasonable patch of open water. Slowly the two had starved. Now and then, judging from the pad marks around the place where they had staged their struggle for survival, the two had been attacked by predators, but fortunately nothing larger than the fox had found them and they had lived until that day.

I took the gander home with me. I tried to restore him, to put weight back on his bones. At first he was intractable, hissing and flapping at me each time I went to feed him, but after a time he learned to trust me and accept my attentions. In spite of all I could do, however, death claimed that goose. He was too far gone.

The memory of him remains. It came to my mind that day, in another part of the wilderness, as I sat among the maples and watched as the geese flew high on their journey to the southland.

The Snake-Neck

The old bull alligator lies submerged, immobile. Only his protuberant nostrils and his eyes with their bony casings show above the dark waters of the everglades. He lies in the lee of a hammock, an area he knows well, where the moving shadows of cypress and live oak combine with the ripples on the water to offer a hiding place in which to wait for prey.

Around the 'gator, in the trees and sloughs and among the coarse saw grass of the glades, the sounds of June supply a medley reminiscent of the jungle: creaks and groans and deep whistles, the splash of jumping fish, the croaking of frogs, the drone of insects. These things combine with the Spanish moss festooning the trees, to give character to this timeless, marshy land. But the sounds and sights of bustling life cannot hide the lurking presence of death.

The bull alligator has been patient this morning, for he is not yet fully hungry and he knows from years of stealthy living that stillness and patience will, sooner or later, furnish him with a meal. Twice already he has almost struck.

The first time a purple gallinule came walking over the lily pads that clustered near the shore, its yellow legs with their long toes stilting gracefully as the green-backed, purple-necked marshbird bobbed along, emitting harsh, hen-like calls. But the gallinule spotted the alligator and took flight, screaming its alarm and showing its white undertail feathers. The alligator remained immobile.

Some time later a water rat slipped into the slough from

Anhinga, also known as snake-bird or water-turkey

another small island and seemed to be going to swim right into the saurian's waiting jaws, only to change course and disappear into a cluster of grasses.

Now it was noon, and the heat of the sun seemed to lull the glades into a rare time of quiet: a few sleepy calls, the occasional flutter of wings, the soft sound of a breeze slipping through the tree-tops. Then, in silence, a strange flotilla rounded the southern point of the alligator's hammock.

Five snakelike necks pushed through the water, sending lazy wavelets in their van. The anhinga family was hunting, the adult birds having brought their three young to this quiet place where they could develop their fishing skills. Already several fish had been speared by the rapier-like beaks of the adults and the chicks had learned to submerge themselves and swim underwater in search of gar or bass.

As the family neared the hammock, one of the young birds broke from the formation and slipped under the water. Not a sound, not a splash accompanied the bird's disappearance, for, like the grebes, anhingas have the ability to expel air from their air sacs and thus sink quietly. The adult birds and the remaining chicks continued swimming, their course parallel to the alligator.

Under the murky water the inexperienced chick paddled quietly with his webbed feet as he turned his head from side to side, seeking fish or snake or frog at which to dart his spearlike beak. He headed directly for the patient alligator. A small garfish shot through the water ahead of the anhinga. The young bird flashed forward and thrust at the fish, his spear embedding itself in the scaly side of the gar. In triumph, the chick surfaced, grasping his prize in his bill.

Instantly the alligator struck, his great jaws engulfing bird and fish. A swirl of water, a sharp, clapping sound, and the 'gator swallowed as he settled back to wait. With a great splashing and venting of their raucous calls, the adult anhingas led their surviving young away from this place of death, swimming swiftly towards their nesting site, a moss-draped oak on a nearby hammock.

Eleven weeks earlier, the male anhinga had half finished a loose nest of sticks and dead leaves in the fork of the live oak; then he had perched on top of it and performed his courting ritual, seeking to attract a female to his new home-site. Standing in the morning sunlight, the male spread his tail feathers and showed off his long black neck, bending it first into an S and then into a U. Uttering hoarse cries and whistling notes, he stretched out first one wing and then the other, so that the silver patches on them shone in the sun. As he made his third deep bow, a female anhinga checked her passing flight and landed on the branches of a nearby tree, watching. At once the male bird redoubled his antics and strutted a little, almost falling off his branch in his eagerness to please and coax the female. Now he began to move his long neck in sweeping arcs, his bill pointed directly at the lady of his attentions, while he ruffled his feathers and kept up a continuous bowing. At last he was rewarded. The female anhinga returned his bows. The two birds paired and their hoarse grunts during the ensuing nuptial ritual were loud and rapid. They crossed necks, rubbed their bills together, and preened each other's feathers, and at last they turned to finish building the nest.

By this time other anhingas were completing their courting rites and the great blue herons were similarly engaged, so that the area was full of harsh sounds and the trees began bulging with huge, untidy nests.

When the nest was completed the female anhinga laid four blue-green eggs into the cup, then she and her mate took turns incubating the pale eggs for almost a month. At the end of that time, three of the eggs hatched, and from then on the adult birds devoted all their energies to feeding their naked, voracious children, which soon became covered with down and, later, with feathers.

Back and forth between the nest and the sloughs the adult anhingas took turns to ferry food to their young. Fish, snakes, newly-hatched alligators, all were crammed down the yawning gullets of the ungainly young, which, as the weeks went by, became bolder and stronger, finally scrambling on to the edge of the nest whenever they saw one of their parents flapping in with food. At last the time came for the young to try out their wings. Now, fully fledged and almost as big as their

Anhinga drying its wings

parents, they teetered clumsily about their nest, stumbling over one another and sometimes scrambling frantically in the branches of their tree. Then one of the young birds toppled out, spread his wings and sailed some distance before flopping down into the water, where, surprised, but evidently proud of his achievement, he began calling loudly. The other young birds followed quickly and the family swam away, seeking food.

After the male youngster was eaten by the alligator, the startled birds took refuge for awhile in their nesting tree. Later, when they had recovered from their fright, the parents led the way to another area of the slough and the four settled to their fishing.

Expelling air from his air sacs, the male bird sank all but his neck; he paddled quietly in this way for a moment or two, waving his neck, and then submerged fully. Under the water he propelled himself with his big webbed feet, moving slowly and scanning the water constantly. Soon he saw a gar, a big fish. In an instant the anhinga kicked himself forward with his feet, straightened his neck and darted his beak at the fish, skewering it securely; then he rose to the surface, and made for shore with the fiercely struggling gar.

A smaller fish would have been adroitly turned and swallowed headfirst as soon as the bird surfaced, but this one was too large, so the anhinga took it ashore and pounded it to death against a rock. After the fish ceased to struggle, the male bird swallowed it, gulping and wheezing in his efforts to down the large gar. At last it was gone. The male anhinga was full. He flapped awkwardly off the ground, but recovered his gracefulness once he was fully airborne. Neck outstretched, long tail spread fan-shaped, he winged his way to a nearby cypress where, heavy and ungainly once more, he perched, wings outspread, to digest his meal.

One by one, each anhinga caught its quota of fish and, satisfied, sought a perch in the sun, until by early afternoon the trees were full of dark, snakelike forms, half-dozing with upraised wings.

A hush settled over the everglades as though the whole vast swampland was taking an afternoon nap. The bull alligator crept out of the water and settled himself to doze on the bank.

Cheery Black-Caps

One summer, a few years ago, while I was out photographing birds, an encounter with a young groundhog triggered into motion a series of thoughts that had been in the back of my mind for some time. They had been put there during a journey in Africa.

I had met a man who earned his living guiding safaris on hunting trips, sightseeing tours and photographing expeditions, and after we became well acquainted in the only habitable hotel in Luanda, the capital of Portuguese Angole, in southwest Africa, he elected to come with me on a three-week trip, as a companion rather than a paid guide.

One morning, as we sat sipping hot, sweet tea on the edge of the Kalahari desert, Bob made a comment that startled me.

"The thing that wild animals fear the most is the human voice," he said, apropos of a discussion we had had the night before.

The statement was flat, authoritative. At that time I had not quite the same amount of experience of the wilderness and its inhabitants as I have now, and I let it pass with but a small argument. Bob's position seemed impregnable and in the end I merely bowed to what I felt must be his superior knowledge of wild animals. Yet his remark stayed with me, worrying me in an indefinable way, and I worked at it on and off as the years slipped by.

Then, as I was walking through a piece of Canadian woodland with my cameras and other picture-taking paraphernalia,

---

Black-capped chickadee

I was startled by a thin, plaintive whistle that was coming from a pile of rocks just ahead. When I stopped, the whistle came again—a soft, almost cooing sound. I searched the rocks and soon spotted the whistler, a rotund young groundhog that stood bolt upright, arms and hands pressed against its sides, as it examined this invader of its domain. Perhaps because it was so close to its burrow it showed no fear, only curiosity.

I whistled back. The little woodchuck put its head on one side, examined me soberly and whistled again. Now I spoke to it, softly; it registered more interest. On such trips I rarely travel without seed and peanuts in one pocket and bread in another, to dispense to those wild things that I meet along the way. Now I dug out some bread, broke off a piece and flipped it towards the groundhog, the while talking quietly. After a sniff or two, the groundhog dropped onto all fours, took the two or three steps needed to reach the bread and began to eat, now and then pausing to study me and to listen to my voice.

I don't know what it was about that groundhog that jolted my memory back to the mist-shrouded morning in the Kalahari, but the retrospect was swift and vivid. I might have been squatting in front of the campfire drinking the scalding tea out there in southwest Africa, instead of standing on the grass of another continent.

"The thing that wild animals fear the most is the human voice." Bob's words returned so clearly that I almost looked around, expecting to see his lanky, sunburned figure standing at my elbow. Now I knew that he had been hopelessly wrong; I knew that despite his great knowledge of the game that he hunted, he had committed the error of generalization. I was sure of this because for years my voice had helped me to instill confidence in wild animals. I had used it again and again, often talking nonsense, for the words didn't matter, just the tone of voice—quiet, confident, soothing. But, of course, I wasn't a hunter; I did not intend to kill and my whole person reflected peaceful intentions.

My friend, on the other hand, was a professional killer. He was a humane man and a brave one, a man who respected

The chickadee is easily tamed.

the game he hunted and who always went after the wounded to put them out of their misery—but he was a killer neverthe- less. His manner reflected it. In the bush he was the arch- predator, keen, intelligent, intense, his nerves stretched taut. His voice, when he used it, was edged with the excitement of the chase. The animals that he hunted recognized the signs and they feared that human voice; they heeded the predatory urges issuing from the vocal cords of the killer. Thus would the impala fear the rasping cough of the hunting leopard.

As I watched the little groundhog nibbling bread, these thoughts tumbled through my mind, and as though by previ- ous appointment, a small bird came to confirm my thinking. The chickadee was one of a flock of some thirty such birds that through autumn and winter and into early spring had spent most of their time around the log house on my forest property, waiting for me to feed them by hand.

Each time I went outside, they would fly to me, landing on my head and shoulders, calling stridently until I produced crushed peanuts or sunflower seeds. Then, once the food was on my extended hand, they would (in strict "pecking order", the strongest bird first) alight on my hand one at a time, take their morsel of seed or peanut and fly off to eat.

The chickadees would talk to me and I to them. Neither of us, of course, understood the speech of the other, yet we communicated by the sound of our voices and by the inflection of the syllables we uttered. I learned the meaning of the various calls made by the small, perky chickadees; they knew the inflections of my voice.

When I called to them my voice would be soft, but audible for some distance, and the birds knew I was disposed to feed them. They would hear me and see me from as far away as 300 or 400 yards and would launch their black and white and gray bodies into air and fly directly to me, tiny bobbing things that unerringly landed on my outstretched hand. At times, just to test them, I would stuff sunflower seeds into my open mouth and hang my hands by my sides. The birds would perch on my lower lip or on my teeth, and pick seeds from within my mouth. And they were all wild birds; none of them had been hand-reared by me.

Sometimes these birds would follow me for a considerable distance through the forest, calling and coming to get food, and then pausing on some branch while they anchored the large sunflower seed with one toe and pecked at it, neatly splitting away the husk. At times they would become almost a nuisance and I would try to ignore their plaintive calls, only to relent as they persisted. Then I would stop, dig seed out of my pocket and say, with feigned impatience, "Oh, come on then, hurry up!" At once, two or three or more would hop onto my person, there to wait while the "boss" bird got his or her seed first.

Now and then, when I was accompanied by people who were not familiar with my birds, they would view my sudden stop and apparently senseless remark with incredulity, believing that I had become affected by the "loneliness" of the forest. When a chickadee responded to my voice, right out of

Chickadee feeding from the author's hand

the wilderness, their incredulity mounted. And when, upon my insistence, they put seeds in their own hand and offered them to the birds, they were invariably delighted that these little wildlings would trust them also. Afterwards they would ask me how I knew that the birds were there, waiting for my call, and at first I would be impatient with such questions, for they, too, had they troubled to listen, could have picked out the voices of these birds from the quiet bustle of the wilderness. But then I would remember that there was a time when the sounds of the forest had no particular meaning for me, either. So I would explain.

If I have such a thing as a favorite bird, it must be the chickadee! I have met them all over the continent and they always gladden the heart. They are, in my view, the most trusting of all the birds, and they are among the most agile and enduring, braving the northland winters when few others their size can survive.

Imagine a creature weighing no more than two ounces, picking a living by searching the frosted trees in temperatures thirty and forty degrees below zero, to find minute, dormant insects! They face blizzards and prolonged periods of terrible cold equipped only with the ability to puff out their feathers for insulation and the keenest little black eyes imaginable. They hop assiduously from branch to branch all the day long, picking, picking, picking, unable to stop in case they do not take in enough protein to allow them to survive the bitter cold of a northern night.

There are six distinct species of chickadee in North America, all of which are about the same size and bear enough of a resemblance to each other to allow for instant recognition. Perhaps the best known is the black-capped, which has a black bonnet and bib that contrast with the white on each side of its head. Its back is olive-gray, and its wings and tail are black edged with white. The underbody is white tinged with buff at the sides.

The chickadee lives almost anywhere, in mixed woods, in evergreen forests, in open places where there is enough cover for its needs. Nesting is done in a cavity. The birds may use an abandoned woodpecker hole or they may excavate their own nesting hole in a decaying stump. The nest is often low to the ground. For nesting material the chickadee picks up such items as discarded animal hair, old feathers, moss, decayed leaves, even spider webs. When the nest is finished the female lays from five to eight eggs, dull white, spotted with reddish-brown, and incubates them for about thirteen days. After the young hatch, both the adult birds spend most of their time feeding their ever-hungry brood. Some three weeks later the hatchlings are ready to fly and although they still demand food from their parents, they soon begin to find their own as the adults leave them for longer and longer periods of time. Anything is food for the chickadee at all seasons; seeds, insects, insect eggs, grubs, chrysalids, meat pilfered from the kills of carnivorous animals, all is grist to the chickadee's mill.

Scream in the Night

I once read a book that described the horned owl's voice as a series of deep *whoo, whoo* notes. The writer went on to explain that there are often five of these deep notes—"also a scream". How very true this is! But that short phrase cannot possibly describe the terrifying sound that results when a great horned owl cuts loose with his banshee wail!

Imagine yourself in the deep forest with a young companion, observing a small clearing at night. The clearing has been baited with ripe fish in the hope of attracting a black bear, which is to be photographed. The young man, a teenager, is the son of a friend and passionately interested in nature, though he has had little opportunity as yet to get into the woods and observe at first hand. So father asks, son pleads, and mother agrees on the promise that the apple of her eye will be tenderly safeguarded.

Off we trudge, equipped with camera, flash unit, some coffee in a thermos, and sandwiches. It is 9:30 at night in mid-July and the mosquitoes are only partly kept at bay with repellent. The moon is full, but clouds obscure it for a time. The forest resounds with night noises: crickets, bullfrogs, whip-poor-wills, nighthawks, and now and then the dry, crackling sound made by some small mammal, a raccoon perhaps, or a porcupine, as he moves about on the ground or in the tree branches.

As we walk, cautiously because I do not wish to use a flashlight, we talk quietly.

Great horned owl

"Now, when we get to the bait area, absolutely no talking and you must keep still. If that bear hears us he'll take off and that'll be that," I instructed.

"O.K." Is the answer a little nervous? We walk a few more steps.

"Why can't we use the flashlight?"

I chuckle quietly, pat the boy's shoulder reassuringly, for there is apprehension in his voice.

"If we use a light, switching it on and off, our eyes won't get used to the darkness. It's better in the bush at night to walk slowly and allow your feet to 'see' for you. They will, you know! I can't explain it, but you sort of feel with your feet, once you get the hang of it. After a while your eyes will pick out objects that are in the way."

We are almost there. I stop, putting my hand on his arm.

"O.K. From now on, not a word. If he doesn't come in a couple of hours, we'll head back—unless you want to stay out here all night?"

"No! A couple of hours will do," the boy says. Then, after a pause: "In a way, I kinda hope it doesn't come!"

So I explain that I have been feeding this bear since spring, and that if we just sit still and let him have a feed, then take the picture, he'll simply go on his way. I feel the lad is reassured, so we walk a little farther, find a good spot by some boulders about thirty feet from the ripe fish, and settle down, making ourselves as comfortable as possible.

Presently the moon peeps from behind a cloud. The forest comes alive with silver light and gently-moving shadows. The sounds of dark continue.

The arrival of the great horned owl is noticed because the big bird appears to slip as it lands in the branches of a nearby pine, else we would hear nothing, for, like all owls, it has softened margins on its wing feathers and its flight is almost totally silent. These things are explained to the boy, mouth close to ear, voice an inaudible whisper. He is warned that the big owl will almost certainly call. We wait.

Soon the owl's deep *whoo, whoos* spill out into the night. The boy listens, fascinated. I am watching the place where the game trail empties into the clearing. From there the bear will come, walking quietly on his fleshy pads, surprisingly quietly for one of such bulk. The boy is looking up at the pine, trying to get a glimpse of the owl.

At last I see a dark, shaggy shape standing at the mouth of the game trail. I am about to nudge the boy, so he can watch the bear's approach, when the owl cuts loose with its great scream.

"Ohmigod!" The boy's exclamation is loud and high pitched. His start is so violent that the thermos and flashlight fall off the rock. The bear whoofs, perhaps as startled as the boy, turns his fat rump and disappears into the night. The boy clutches my arm and I try to tell him it is only the owl, but laughter wells out of me and that is probably the best medicine for a young man's frazzled nerves. In any event the vigil is ended. We retrieve the fallen items. The flashlight is broken, but the thermos is intact. So we drink a cup of coffee and I explain about the owl's dreadful scream.

"It is intended to startle, you see, to make a hare or a woodchuck jump, revealing itself to the owl's big eyes. Often these animals, if they become suspicious, will 'freeze', becoming completely immobile and fading into their background, and then the owl is not just sure where they are. So it yells and watches for the reaction," I tell the boy.

An afterthought occurs to me: "It's just as well your mother wasn't here, or she'd be having a fit about now."

"And just what do you think I'm having?" The boy's reply is serious enough, yet there is an underlying sense of humor coming to the rescue. We walk on, coffee finished, and I tell him more about owls.

Why are people so often startled by owls? After thinking about this for some time, I have concluded that it is not the bird itself, or even its voice, of which people are afraid, but rather the circumstances under which they hear the call and the suddenness of the call itself. Most of those who jump at the sound of an owl in the dark forest or night field, are strangers in a new world; they face the world of the animals, knowing little about it, and they hear magnified all the small

sounds of the night. A mouse rustling through the grass becomes transformed into a monster; the breeze that stirs the tree-tops, now and then sending a dead twig crackling down to the forest floor, is interpreted as a threat. Apprehension sets in as the imagination gallops into strange places. At such a moment the sudden call of an owl is likely to cause the flesh to creep and the hair to prickle on the nape of the neck.

Of course, owls are completely harmless to all but the small creatures upon which they prey. They are, indeed, beneficial to nature as whole, for they play an important part in keeping down the numbers of rodents that, unchecked, would overrun field and forest.

Owls are found throughout the world and although they vary in plumage, size, voice and habitat, they share many of the same characteristics. They are predominantly night hunters endowed with very large eyes (the eyes of most owls are larger than those of an adult human) and they have the gift of silent flight because of those muffled wing edges.

Either because they swallow more fur and feathers or because their digestion is not as effective, owls regurgitate more pellets than do hawks. Often, when an owl habitually roosts in the same tree day after day, these cast pellets, molded by a digestive system that rejects all but the flesh of the bird's prey, provide an easy way to get a good look at an owl. By diligently searching the foot of large, likely-looking "owl" trees, such as tall pines or maples, one may find a large number of these pellets; then, a careful scrutiny of the tree's branches will often reveal the sleeping bird.

In addition, if these pellets are gathered and dissected, the bones and teeth they contain afford valuable clues to the feeding habits of the bird. Scientific examination of pellets has shown that hares, rabbits and small rodents are the principal food of all owls.

Owls, by the way, are not blind in daylight. They can see perfectly well at all times, though their great eyes, like those of cats, are designed to capture every last bit of light during their normal feeding hours of night. Some species, that breed

Young great horned owls

in the far north, may hunt by day. This is probably because they encounter extremely long hours of daylight in the arctic summer and if they were to hunt only in the dark they would certainly perish. The snowy owl, for instance, hunts as well by day as by night, and the hawk owl forages exclusively during the hours of light.

Another interesting characteristic of owls is worth mentioning. They have a habit of turning the head slowly in one direction and, when it has turned to its maximum extent, whipping it back so quickly to the other side that early observers credited the owl with being able to swivel its head right around! This is not so, of course, but the facts are remarkable nevertheless. The eyes of owls are immovable in their sockets and to compensate for this, nature has endowed these birds with the ability to turn their head for nearly 180 degrees in either direction, affording almost a complete circle of vision.

Because of their great, staring eyes, their large, hooked beaks, and their sharp talons, owls look fierce and to some people, menacing. In fact they are quite docile birds, and extremely beneficial both to man and to nature by keeping the rodent population in check.

Big Bills

On the ground, the pelican waddles clumsily, a squat and ugly bird whose great beak points downwards, as though the weight of this gross appendage was too much for the comparatively small head. As it essays to fly, it looks even more cumbersome and gives the initial impression that it will fail to lift off, such is the threshing of the long wings and the awkward, feet-together hopping that is characteristic of this bird. But once airborne, it is graceful and dignified as it sails away on slow, sweeping wings.

Sociable birds, pelicans usually fly in V-formation or in a long line. They alternately glide and flap in almost perfect unison, keeping themselves precisely spaced, with necks curved back and great beaks carried horizontally.

Pelicans are the largest of an order of birds that includes cormorants, anhingas, gannets, frigate-birds, tropic-birds and boobies. These birds are all fish eaters and are related because of their feet, which have webs that join all four toes. (Ducks and other water birds have webs that unite only the three front toes.)

Although both species of pelican found in North America feed on fish and have the same large, pouched beak and similar build, there are distinct differences in color, in the manner in which each species feeds and in selection of habitat.

The brown pelican fishes in salt water, diving spectacularly on its prey. It lives on the east and west coasts, from South Carolina and California southward.

The white pelican, the larger of the two species, dwells almost exclusively on inland lakes, though it will also frequent

White pelican

Pelicans flying—a magnificent sight

brackish and salt waters in winter after migration from its breeding range in western Canada and north-central United States. With its orange beak, white plumage and black wing tips, this spectacular bird is readily recognized. Unlike the brown, the white pelican rarely dives for its food, electing instead to swim on the surface in shallow areas, dipping up its prey; at times a group of birds will band together to beat the water with their wings and gulp pouchfuls of the small fish that are stirred up in this way. It has a wing span of up to ten feet, about a foot wider than its brown relative.

The brown pelican, while less spectacular in color, is remarkable for its dives for food, when it may plunge headfirst into the sea from a height of seventy-five feet, after coasting along for a time watching for a school of fish. Sighting its prey, the pelican suddenly tips its body forward, half closes its wings and dives, its long beak pointing straight down and its body rotating as it falls. This bird has a number of air sacs just under the skin, which help to cushion the shock of impact with the water and then act as a "life jacket" to bring the bird back up to the surface as swiftly and lightly as a cork. Although to date there is no proof that the brown pelican is able to keep its bearings while below the surface, it is often seen to dive downwind—against the direction of take-off—and rotate its body under water to emerge facing upwind, ready to rise into the air anew.

The pouch of a pelican is not a storage bin for its food. It serves merely as a scoop in which to catch the fish the bird hunts and it must be drained of water before the pelican can swallow its catch. To do this, the bird lets the water out between its mandibles by moving its head sideways and slightly downwards; then, when the pouch is empty of water, it tilts up its head and lets the fish slide down its gullet.

The capacity of the pouch, which may vary between birds, appears to be between three and four gallons of liquid. At ten pounds weight per gallon, this makes an impressive load for the bird to haul up from under the water, particularly when this burden is added to by the weight of the fish that the bird has captured.

The pouch has at least one more use—as a receptacle for

the "soup," on which the newly-hatched young are fed. This is a regurgitated mixture of fish and fish juices. The adults swallow their catches as soon as they make them and by the time they get back to the nest, their fast-acting digestive enzymes have begun to work on the fish. As the young pelicans grow and their beaks become long, they begin to thrust them down the throats of their parents, searching for less-digested fish.

Young white pelicans come into the world from white eggs, laid on a mound of vegetation that the adults have raked up in some marshy area. They are pink and naked and have short, rubbery beaks, but by the time they are two weeks old they are decently clothed in white down.

Brown pelicans build their nests of sticks, either on the ground or in the forks of trees. By five weeks the babies can waddle about the nesting area, if they are born in a ground nest; but those born in trees stay put, at best just shuffling within their nesting cup until they are ready to fly.

Pelicans rarely make a noise when adult, appearing to rely on visual communication when fishing and flying. They do occasionally make croaking sounds, and antics such as beak-clacking and neck- and head-posturing may also provide some form of communication, particularly during the mating season.

Pelicans nest usually in large colonies. These can be noisy places, for, unlike their almost silent parents, young pelicans clamor energetically for their food, making strange, bleating sounds.

Brown pelican

Mighty Midget

It was spring in the Ontario northwoods. I had walked for some two hours and then decided to sit on a downed tree to contemplate the forest and listen to the sounds of the birds, feeling that special contentment that only the freedom of the wilderness can give. Presently, the ringing cry of a pileated woodpecker intruded on my thoughts. The bird was nearby and I got up from my seat to catch a glimpse of the cock-of-the-north, the beautiful, crow-sized tree borer with the flaming red crest. I walked on, slowly, absorbing the sights, listening to the sounds of the awakening wilderness.

Since dawn I had been following a game trail that wound through stands of mixed woods: hemlock and spruce, with poplar and birch filling the gaps left by the felling of trees. Soon the trail led me into a small, natural clearing. The grass that grew on it was inviting. I felt lazy; I stretched out, my back to the ground, and watched the sky. It was one of those days—you know the kind—when the sun is hot and the blue sky is lightly hazed by thin clouds.

As I watched, I picked out the shape of a large buteo as it circled slowly overhead, wings unmoving. Lazily I raised my field glasses and instantly saw, illuminated in fine detail by the early morning sun, the reddish underparts and the wide black bands on the tail that identified it as a red-shouldered hawk. It planed along, using thermal updrafts, making its show of aerobatics look simple as it went through the rituals

Ruby-throated hummingbird

A perfect fit

of its courting flight. Soon it rose in tight spirals, became a tiny speck, and was gone.

The sky was empty again. I lay still, entirely relaxed, feeling the warmth of the earth, smelling the aroma of hot soil as it mixed with the fragrance of the grasses.

Idle thoughts chased each other through my mind, soft, lazy thoughts, and I realized suddenly that the flight of the hawk with its easy, graceful sweep, had helped me relax after a long week in the turbulent city. From my position on the ground I could hear the sounds of life around me: the droning of a bee, the dry rustle of a dragonfly's wings, the breeze sweeping along the tops of the grasses. Without conscious effort my body became completely relaxed, blending of its own accord into the contours of the earth.

I just watched the sky. Clouds, white and dimpled and round, passed in leisurely manner across the blue above. Four turkey vultures glided into view. Did they believe me dead? They seemed to give me more than just passing attention, moving their bare, red heads from side to side as they circled above me, scanning my shape with their magnificently keen sight. But no, they knew there was life down here. Executing beautiful maneuvers, they left.

Came two chickadees and a crow. The small birds, like fighter planes pursuing a heavy bomber, were harassing the black marauder, which must have passed too close to their nest. The three disappeared from my circle of vision and for awhile the sky was open, a blue expanse with not even a small cloud now to spoil its pastel color.

Presently I heard the whirring of quick wings, and a tiny, glittering bird passed swiftly over me not more than four feet from the ground. A ruby-throated hummingbird! I sat up to watch it, the spell now broken; the naturalist came alive.

I watched the bird, a female, as she hovered over a small, stunted spruce tree, and I marveled at her grace and speed and endurance. If a 160-pound man tried to copy the behavior of this less-than-one-ounce bird, he would need to burn 145,000 calories every day and his body would evaporate some ninety pounds of water; if he did not replace his lost moisture quickly enough his skin temperature would rise so high that he would probably burst into flames!

Yet this tiny bird with a taste for sweetness manages a series of feats that are as incredible as they are graceful. No other avian species flies quite like the hummingbird. It can hover in mid-air or move upwards, forwards or backwards with equal facility, its wings moving so rapidly they are just a swift blur.

To get its food, the hummingbird uses a long, thin bill and a tube-like tongue that can stretch out at least a couple of inches. With these tools and aided by its speed of flight—up to to thirty miles an hour in "high gear"—it hovers at flowers and consumes a daily ration of nectar, spiders and small insects, that amounts to half of its own weight. Because hummingbirds are so fast and so small, they must constantly replenish the energy that they burn faster than any other bird or mammal. This causes them to feed every ten or fifteen minutes of the day, sipping nectar or adroitly catching insects in flight.

Another remarkable characteristic of these little birds is their ability to go into a semi-torpid condition at night. In this way they conserve body energy, because their metabolism slows down to about one-twentieth of its normal, extremely high rate.

Small though they are—scarcely more than three inches long—ruby-throated hummingbirds migrate as much as 2,000 miles from their breeding grounds, as far north as southern Canada, to their winter range in southern Texas and northern Mexico, southern Alabama and Florida, even crossing the Gulf of Mexico to South America.

Watching the female bird that morning, I noticed that she made several trips to the stunted spruce tree; I wondered if her nest was located inside its shelter, so I used my field glasses and kept the tree in focus. The bird appeared, hovered for a moment, then disappeared into the tree's twisted branches. As I walked towards the tree, the bird emerged and whirred away. For some time I stood below the spruce, gazing up into its branches in search of the nest, but I had to climb the tree before I finally located the tiny cup about twelve feet from the ground. Even then I doubt whether I would have found it had not one of the young birds raised its thin neck and bulbous head, perhaps believing that the movement of the branches heralded the return of its food-bearing mother.

The nest was about the size of a whole walnut, set on end. It was marvelously built. Lichens, mosses, thistledown and wispy fibers had been used in its weaving, and it was anchored to a forked branch by spider webs. Inside the inch-deep cup nestled two small birds—the usual hummingbird family—about an inch long and already partly fledged, but with beaks not yet fully developed. Quietly I descended and waited near the tree to watch the mother make a few more trips to feed her young. I wondered at the skill with which she thrust her long, needle-like bill down the throats of those minute nestlings without injuring their delicate membranes. I admired the iridescent, greenish sheen of her back, which contrasted with the white throat and underparts. Had she been a male her throat feathers would have glowed ruby-red, but even so she shone like a jewel in the sun.

I watched, spellbound, and waited, hoping for a glimpse of the male bird, but apparently he was fully occupied else-where. Perhaps he had discovered a patch of milkweed or honeysuckle and was feasting on the nectar that he found there. At any rate, he did not appear, and after half an hour I gave up and continued my walk through the woods.

Noisy Flyers

An hour after leaving the hummingbirds' nest I was threading my way through an area densely packed with young maple trees, following a thin game trail. Suddenly the trail led
me into a small, rock-strewn clearing and there, scooting
along like a tiny, animated toy, was a young killdeer. It was
black and white and buffy and had legs that seemed too long
for such a small bird; and how it could run, that small bundle
of downy life!

I had already been made aware, by the behavior of the parent birds, that somewhere on this open stretch of land there
was either a nest containing eggs, or young birds. I knew
from experience that it was almost hopeless to seek the chicks
once they had been alerted by the cries of their parents, for
they blend so well into their background and move so quickly and stealthily that if they are occasionally seen it is more
by accident than by design. But now I had caught one of the
young birds in the open, where only bare rock was to be
found. A crouching killdeer chick, as still as a statue, is a
hard thing to detect; but this one had evidently become sepa-
rated from its nest mates and now it flashed away from me on
its spindly legs, uttering its high-pitched call of alarm.

Around me, meanwhile, the parent birds were shrieking
warnings to their young. Their cries were intended to achieve
two things: to urge the chicks to extra caution and to attract
the attention of the intruder from the young to themselves.
Now and then one or the other of the adult birds would land

Killdeer

near me, pretending injury and going through antics intended to fool a predator into believing that an easy meal was to be had for the taking.

I refused to allow them to distract me. I had brought a camera along, and I determined to photograph the young killdeer if I could get it to remain still for long enough. Its picture would make up for the camera's inability to capture the images of the two nestling hummingbirds, whose nest had been in so much shadow that photographing them had been impossible. So I kept my eyes glued on the small bird. It had slowed its frantic run off the granite and had reached the grasses and wild strawberry plants that bordered the rock. As I stood still and watched the fledgling killdeer, using the field glasses, it stopped, stood immobile, and then slowly crouched down. It was as well that I had kept the glasses trained on it, else it would have disappeared completely from my sight. Even with the glasses, all that I could see was the outline of its head and the dark, pointed shape of its beak. I mentally marked the spot and walked slowly towards it.

The parent birds were a nuisance. They kept coming closer and their constant shrieking was distracting. Often I was tempted to take my eyes from the spot where their chick was crouched, which was, of course, their intention. At last I was within some fifteen feet of the young bird. I stopped. Its shape was clear through the 200-millimeter lens of my camera. I focused and took two pictures, then I moved three feet nearer. The chick remained still. I took two more photographs and moved closer yet. Now the telephoto lens had to be switched for a normal lens. Working slowly and quietly I changed elements, crouched, and clicked the shutter. Then I leaned forward even closer to the chick and took one last picture.

I glanced down at the camera as I wound the film on, then looked up again. The chick was gone. Though I had taken enough photographs, I was curious. I tried to find the young killdeer again. It was hopeless. The parents evidently knew their chick was safe, for they redoubled their efforts to distract me and to lead me away from their young. Both adults landed some distance from me and began the broken-wing

Killdeer "nest"

ritual, flopping around on the ground in pretense of injury, only to recover suddenly when I approached, then to land some distance further and go through their act all over again. I turned away, leaving the birds alone, and continued my walk.

Killdeer belong to the family Charadriidae, which includes plovers and turnstones, and they are by far the best known and the most widely distributed members of this family in North America. The name of the species, *Charadrius vociferus*, is most apt, for killdeer spend much of their time on the wing emitting their high-pitched calls—*killdee, killdee, killdee*—from which their common name has been derived.

Although classed as shorebirds, killdeer are just as likely to be found inland, even in natural clearings in the deeper woods, though most commonly in open country. A killdeer's nest is hardly worthy of the name, for it is merely a slight hollow in the ground, or, at best, a depression surrounded by a few small stones or some grass stems, in which the female deposits four buffy eggs that are blotched and spotted with black. Both birds share in the job of incubating the eggs, from which the young hatch about twenty-five days later.

Killdeer, like all shorebirds, begin life fully dressed in down and are perfectly able to run and feed and hide just as soon as they are dry. When they attain adult plumage their markings are distinct, beginning with a brownish, pigeon-like beak, a brown and white head followed by an immaculate white collar, then a jet black band around the neck, another, but partial, white necklace and another black band. On the back and above the wings, the birds are predominantly brown. Their underparts are white.

Like all plovers, killdeer are expert flyers, as graceful and agile in the air as on the ground. As they wheel restlessly over some stony meadow we see the flash of buffy red on the rump which is distinctive of their species. The long tail contributes to their length of ten inches, and they have a wingspread of twice that measure.

Death on the Lake

The big turtle is almost buried in the slime of the lakebed. His moss-covered shell looks like a large, green rock; he is motionless, and hungry. Inches above, on the surface of the water, a mallard duck paddles gently towards the submerged reptile, now and then dipping her head under the water, her pointed tail lifting upwards as she reaches with her beak for the foods that are hidden in the murk of the shallows. The snapping turtle watches her with unwinking black eyes, his horny, triangular head arched up.

Elsewhere in the vicinity, life sleeps, lulled into quiet by the heat of the summer noon. Grandpappy Lake, they call the small body of water that is round like a giant's spit droplet carelessly expectorated into one tiny hollow of the vast wilderness. Now and then sunlight reflected from the still surface of the water casts a fleeting, golden shaft on the untidy beaver lodge that nestles under the shade of a spruce tree. A red-winged blackbird flies low over the water. It lands on a branch in the spruce and eyes the duck.

The blackbird sings, *konk-aree,* its liquid trill strangely haunting. Now it is quiet. It peers about, then preens, spreading one black wing with its scarlet shoulder patch. The bird watches as the duck moves closer to the turtle.

The mallard's orange feet, their webs outstretched to form small paddles, almost brush the green moss growing on the reptile's back, and the turtle's horny snout is poised to strike.

The mallard is now almost over the turtle's head. She moves forward another couple of inches. The predatory beak

under the water streaks upwards, and the horny vise clamps on the mallard's right foot.

The duck utters one startled cry, and she fights. Her flapping wings and jerking body send small shock waves rippling over the glass-still surface of the water. In her struggle the mallard loses some of her flight feathers. They float near her for a moment, then they are pushed away by the waves raised by the frantic wings.

The turtle hangs on to the duck's foot. He is an old and experienced hunter and he uses his great weight to anchor the mallard, patient and unconcerned over his victim's frenzies. Nothing can now rob him of his meal. Nothing? The foot is fragile; it could snap off and the wounded mallard could yet be able to scuttle away from him. The turtle waits for the right moment and when the duck sinks down under the water, momentarily exhausted by her wild fight, he shifts his grip higher up the leg.

A beaver floats to the surface near his house of sticks and mud, made curious by the noises of the duck's struggles. He must cruise out to see what is causing this sudden disturbance. His dark brown, furry head cuts through the water in a smooth arc as he circles the mallard, sees, and is satisfied. He swims back to his lodge, pausing a moment to smack his wide tail against the surface of the water, signaling his displeasure with those who have disturbed his noon sleep; then he dives, slipping back into the cool chamber of his lodge. The plight of the mallard is of no consequence to him.

In the spruce tree overhead the blackbird has stopped preening his feathers and is watching the battle with one eye, his small head cocked to one side. He notes the floating feathers and he wonders if he will find some particle of meat or fat attached to their ends. No, the feathers can wait. The red-wing knows that soon larger pieces of skin and meat will float on the surface, so he stays on his perch, waiting.

An hour has passed. The mallard's lunges for freedom are weaker. The turtle drags the duck's head under the water more often and he can now hold it for several seconds at a

A pair of mallards

time, until with her last strength the captive duck arches up again for a quick gasp of air. Working slowly and with great patience, the turtle moves his hold higher and now he has a good grip on the duck's thigh. Already a large section of the mallard's soft belly skin has ripped and blood is tinging the water.

Death hovers near. Others besides the red-wing are waiting for it. A school of sunfish has moved in close to the turtle and his victim; the little fish are the lake's scavengers, cleaning up the leftovers of the killers that live in its waters. Sometimes they are themselves prey, but now they know they have nothing to fear from the large turtle. They are excited and impatient. They can taste and smell the kill in the water and one of them slips in to nip at a bit of meat that is trailing from the mallard's torn belly. The little fish grips the meat with his pin-sharp teeth; he pulls, shaking his oval body from side to side, but the meat resists his tug. Still holding on to his prize, he moves closer, then backs away suddenly, shaking his body more violently. The meat rips free. The fish races away with it, pursued by some of the others in the school, who now seek to share that which they were afraid to steal from the predator's jaws. The daring fish gulps as he swims and the meat disappears into his mouth. He is able to finish swallowing before the others reach him and they all turn back, swimming near the turtle, for they are excited by the taste of blood in the water.

The helpless mallard is exhausted. She floats on the water, a look of resignation in her eyes. She knows she is doomed. There is no point in fighting any more. But the turtle is patient; he is hungry, yet he will not risk losing his meal through haste. He continues his mangling hold and enjoys the taste of it, like a gourmet slowly savoring a rare dish. Then he begins to back slowly towards deeper water, dragging the mallard with him, submerging her head more frequently.

At last it is done. The duck's body jerks suddenly, and is still. Her neck hangs; her green, black-tipped beak rests limply on the bottom. Still the turtle waits.

Above, in the spruce tree, the blackbird trills again, seem-

A flock of carefree males

ing to voice his impatience with the turtle's caution. From his perch the bird can see the outline of the big shell that is clouded by drifting ooze; he can see the red life that has escaped the duck's body, its stain deeper as it hangs around the turtle.

Tentatively, the big reptile releases his crushing hold. Nothing happens. The duck is dead; the meal is ready. Taking hold of the leg again, the turtle drags the carcass deeper into the water and chooses a flat sandy shelf upon which to eat his meal. The sunfish rush to the kill and begin feeding in frantic haste. Pieces of meat float to the surface.

The blackbird flies down from his perch. Skimming low over the water, the bird picks up a piece of meat; he flies back to the tree, picks at his find, then drops it and returns for a new piece. The meat the bird has dropped lodges in the tree's scaly bark; the ants find it, and it turns black with their feeding shapes.

The lake is asleep again. Soon evening will come with a breeze that will wake its surface and bring out the other ducks that are quacking sleepily in the reeds. They will come in noisy flotillas, and with their coming the beaver will slip out of their lodge and swim wide circles around the lake, inspecting the shoreline, seeking changes that may tell them of danger. If all is well they will swim ashore, their bodies sleek with moisture, and they will wade clumsily into the shallows, there to feed on water plants and roots.

The sun is gone. A thin, pale moon peeps over the treetops. There is no sign of the day's struggle except a few feathers pressed against the shoreline.

The turtle lies quiet and replete. He will stay submerged until his need for air drives him cumbersomely to the surface, where he will hang, his head just protruding from the water, his small nostrils snuffling at the night.

In the spruce the blackbird is asleep. He sits balanced on a high branch with his head buried under one wing. Now and then he utters a small chirping sound.

Scarlet and Gold

Spring came slowly to my farm that year and the migrant birds were held back by the chilly weather. Few of the north-ward-bound species had arrived on my 350 acres of mixed woodlands that were linked by several large clearings. It was late April. I had already been searching for new buds and new birds while walking through the woods, eyeing the lingering patches of snow.

As I walked home one evening, I was depressed. I had had enough of winter and I even fell to thinking that if spring did not arrive soon, I would take a trip south, perhaps to the everglades to feel some warm sunshine on my back as I studied the birds and animals of that balmy region. By the time I reached my home, I had decided to give the weather until the end of that week to warm up; if it did not, I would leave.

Having done that, I felt more cheerful, and as I sat over supper in this new frame of mind I suddenly realized I could not bear to carry out my plan. Why, I would be missing the excitement of spring in these northwoods! I would not be here to see the first birds arrive and bustle about their home sites. I would miss the sprouting of small green buds and the sight of pastel-shaded hepaticas and white bloodroot blossoms. So I changed my mind and elected to wait out the cold. And with that I went to bed.

When I got up next morning, the sun was shining clear and strong, the cold north winds had stopped blowing. The transformation had come overnight! Stopping only to wrap a robe around myself and slip my feet into moccasins, I left the

house and at once felt the benign breath of spring. And on my lawn there were three robins!

I walked through a meadow to the maple syrup house, which stood in a rocky clearing that had once been used for pasturing cattle. Growing here and there were some old apple trees, on one of which I saw a profusion of large, yellow blooms! But no, these were not flowers, they were goldfinches, about 100 of them in their bright, spring dress, chattering and scrambling through the branches of the apple tree. Now and then they made short flights to the ground, where they would scratch and forage like a flock of tiny, beautiful chickens.

I was delighted, and last evening's thoughts of Florida were totally banished as I sat on a rock, feeling the warm sun on my bare head and watching the "wild canaries". Then, nothing would do but that I return to the house, get ready, have a quick breakfast and slip away for a good tramp through my property, heading north into government wildlands and to a small lake, five miles distant, which was the spring and summer home of many birds.

By nine o'clock I was away, a small packsack on my back in which were sandwiches and a thermos of coffee. The goldfinches had left the apple tree and were scattered over the clearing, picking up seeds, pecking at insects, singing. I knew they would still be here on my return, and that there would be bright yellow goldfinches in the area of my house all summer and right into the fall. I would have ample opportunity to watch them again.

Half an hour after crossing the boundaries of my property, I heard a cock grouse drum his love song and I stopped to listen for a time; then, from the opposite direction, another cock replied, combining his wooing with a challenge to the rival male. I walked on, feasting on the signs of spring — the newly-awakened insects, the soft spongy ground replete with the moisture of melted snow, the swelling buds on the poplars and birches, the yellow-orange color of the willows that proclaimed the rising of their sap.

American goldfinch

Scarlet tanager

As I walked through a clump of tall poplar trees, I heard a hoarse, buzzing song that I recognized: *queerit, queerit, queery, queery, queer!* I stopped and leaned against a tree, field glasses ready. Somewhere in the trees ahead of me, a newly-arrived scarlet tanager was staking out his territory. Again the bird sang, and then once more. He was close, but despite his scarlet coat I could not find him. I kept the glasses busy, but with no luck, and I was about to walk on, giving up on this elusive fellow, when his voice came from so near that I almost jumped. I put down the glasses and searched with my eyes and there, perched on a branch, not more than fifteen feet away, sat the tanager, glowing in his red dress that contrasted so vividly with the tidy black wings and tail. For a time we looked at each other, then the tanager flitted away, to stop unseen on some other branch and sing his song again and again. I walked on, feeling the fullness of spring and the contentment that is always mine when I walk through the wildwoods.

It was late afternoon when I returned home. The goldfinches were still there, only now there were more of them— three flocks, each busy scratching around the fields and the house yard, tame, happy, beautiful in their yellows and blacks and whites. I had seen other birds that day, of course, but I was especially glad for the goldfinches and the tanager. The finches were not unusual around my home, and they were always there to see, even in winter, but then their yellow was replaced by a dull brownish-olive, and the males did not wear their little black caps. Neither was the tanager rare, but despite his glowing red garb, he was a hard fellow to find in the leafy summer, being somehow able to blend right into the green foliage and disappear from view.

The contrasts between these two birds are many. The tanager, larger, blazing red and less sociable, is a bird of secretive ways; the finches, happy in each other's company, are soft yellow and trusting of man. Distinctly different species with distinctly different ways, but to me, that spring, they were linked because they were the first newcomers to capture my attention and admiration.

Goldfinches are predominantly seed eaters, though, like most birds, they will eat insects when they come across them or when there are no seeds to be had. They are unusually late nesters, waiting to raise their single brood until the thistledown they use for their nests is ripe and cottony, which does not occur until July and August. They romp through the open fields and in the underbrush in happy flocks, singing their pert songs as they fly in undulating course, climbing and dipping. At the top of each rise, they sing their song: *per-chic-o-ree, per-chic-o-ree,* as though urging the seeds of the wild chicory, one of their favorite foods, to hurry up and ripen.

In winter and early spring, goldfinches feed on almost any

139

left-overs from the previous year, including grass seeds, elm seeds and, where they are available, the old apple seeds from last autumn's deadfall fruits. The May-time harvest of dandelion seeds offers special attraction and the birds even pick at tender buds and eat their share of greenery. In June, weed seeds offer abundant feeding. Then, in July, the thistles mature and offer both food and nesting material, and the finches begin to court and make their nests.

When the neat cups are woven out of grasses and fibers and lined with soft thistledown, from two to seven eggs are laid. The young hatch in about two weeks. Then both birds take up the task of feeding the brood on an almost exclusive diet of seeds, which are first husked and swallowed by the parents and then regurgitated in the form of mushy "porridge".

When the fledglings are some sixteen days old, they leave the nest and a few days later are on their own, following their parents and other adults in the ceaseless hunt for food. In the fall, they feel the pull of the south, and the flocks move in that direction. In southern Canada and the northern United States, wintering flocks roam the fields, often in company with redpolls and tree sparrows and other small seed eaters, finding food in the tops of weeds and grasses that project above the snow. Some goldfinches, however, spend the winter as far south as Mexico.

Tanagers generally arrive north of the Canadian border in May, though early arrivals are not unusual. As long as the sun shines warmly, these insect eaters have little trouble in finding their favorite foods in the early spring forests. A little smaller than a robin, slimmer, and with a heavier beak, tanagers are responsible for consuming great quantities of harmful bugs. Such is this bird's appetite for insects that ornithologist Edward H. Forbush once watched two tanagers feeding on gypsy moth caterpillars for eighteen minutes, consuming the insects at the rate of thirty-five caterpillars a minute! Nevertheless, the tanager is also fond of wild fruit and will consume it in considerable amounts when it is available.

During the courting season, the male fluffs up his feathers, cocks his tail in the air, droops his wings rather like a catbird, and sings lustily. Sometimes he gets an answer from his dull, greenish lady, in the form of a coy, low whistle.

The nest is built of twigs, rootlets and grasses and anchored on a branch from ten to fifty feet above the ground. The three or four bluish eggs take about two weeks to hatch. On occasion, tanagers find themselves victims of the cowbird, a member of the blackbird family that, like the European cuckoo, lays its eggs in the nests of other birds, refusing to accept the cares of parenthood.

After the young are raised, the tanagers continue hunting through the woods until September signals the time to fly to South America. In the jungles of that continent, their name originated; it was bestowed upon them by the Tupi Indians of the Amazon, who call them *tangará.*

The Night Flyers

Whip-poor-will, whip-poor-will, whip-poor-will, . . . the chant went on endlessly as the sleek night bird sat lengthwise on the branch of a maple tree that grew on the edge of a clearing. A full moon revealed the shapes of all the trees and highlighted with silver the tops of the wild grasses; the incessant drone of mosquitoes blended with the faint rustling of the leaves.

I listened to the monotonous voice of the whip-poor-will for several minutes, counting each call as it was made. When I reached 569, the bird suddenly stopped, emitted one short *whip,* and then began anew. Presently another took up the call, the pair at times chanting so closely in unison that it sounded like one voice emerging from twin stereo speakers placed some distance apart; then one bird would alter its beat slightly and the two voices would become distinct again, though one slightly overlapped the other.

Because the mosquitoes were plentiful and constantly seeking my blood, I gave up on my count. As I crossed the large clearing, the voice of another bird became audible as a nighthawk flew high overhead, busy at its favorite occupation of insect-hunting. *Peent, peent,* the nasal call was repeated again and again, but at longer intervals than the whip-poor-will's continuous dirge.

Nighthawks and whip-poor-wills both are members of the

Common nighthawk with young

family Caprimulgidae, or goatsuckers. This is a name mistakenly bestowed, that has somehow stuck. In olden days, in England, where members of this family are also found, superstitious farm hands swore that these night birds milked their goats. In reality, the birds were probably flying low, between the grazing animals, picking up insects that the goats' hoofs disturbed, for all the goatsuckers are completely insectivorous. They have very small beaks, but enormous mouths that open right back almost to the ears. With mouth agape, they patrol the air, catching flying insects on the wing.

The name "nighthawk" is, of course, another misnomer. The bird does appear somewhat hawklike when in flight, having a large size, sleek, pointed wings and a longish tail, but there the resemblance ends. In addition to its tiny, unhawklike beak, it has, in common with all its family, short legs and nearly useless little feet that cannot even grasp a perch; as a result, the goatsuckers rest lengthwise on a branch rather than across it, as other birds do.

Even the first half of the nighthawk's name is misleading, for it is as likely to be seen and heard by day as by night. Dusk and dawn seem to be its favorite times to cruise the sky, wheeling and swooping restlessly in pursuit of flying insects.

During the spring courtship, the male nighthawk indulges in a series of spectacular dives. The bird plunges with stiff wings as though he were about to dash himself against the ground, but a few yards before impact he turns his dive into a climb; at the moment of upturn, the wind strums suddenly through his outstretched pinions and produces a sound not unlike that which would result if one stretched a thick elastic band and plucked it.

The whip-poor-will looks very similar to the nighthawk, but is distinguished by its shorter wings and its rounded tail. At rest, a nighthawk's wings reach up to, or beyond, the end of the tail, while those of the whip-poor-will do not. In flight, the nighthawk's tail is forked and there is a white patch under each wing, while the whip-poor-will's wings appear uni-

Whip-poor-will

formly dark. If one has a very close view of the birds, it can be seen that the nighthawk is "clean-shaven", whereas the whip-poor-will has a definite fringe of hairlike feathers around its mouth, which helps the bird scoop up insects in flight.

Nighthawks and whip-poor-wills are ground "nesters" that do not bother to build a nest. Perhaps, because the birds are themselves so well camouflaged, they do not wish to attract notice to their eggs and young by constructing a proper nest. Instead they pick a spot on the ground, into which their mottled plumage will blend so completely that one may pass within a yard or two of a sitting bird without seeing it. Both species lay two eggs that are blotched and spotted with various colors, making them hard to locate; and when they hatch, the young are covered with grayish or brownish down which provides excellent camouflage.

There is one other characteristic that is shared by the goatsucker family: that of almost noiseless flight, made possible by the softness of their feathers. Whether this is of any value to their hunting is not known. Owls, of course, prey largely on mammals, and thus find advantage in their silent flight, but one does not think of insects as being too sensitive to sound.

The nighthawk has a very wide distribution, ranging over open country across the continent from about the latitude of James Bay, south to Mexico and the Gulf. It winters in South America.

The whip-poor-will is found in woodlands east of the Rockies, from southern Canada to Georgia and Louisiana, spending the winter in the southeastern United States and south to Central America.

The western counterpart of the whip-poor-will is the poorwill, a smaller, grayer bird which nests on the arid plains. Another North American goatsucker is the chuck-will's-widow, which breeds in low-lying areas in the southeastern and south-central States, wintering in southern Florida and southward. It is larger and browner than the whip-poor-will, with almost no white in its plumage.

Diogenes

Those of you who have never had a fat, partly-digested earthworm regurgitated into your ear by a loving young crow, just don't know what you're missing—which is just as well! I can tell you from personal experience that the ensuing warm and pulpy mess packed vigorously into your ear hole by a strong and pointed beak is painful and makes rather repulsive little sounds as it is going in. In addition, it is difficult to extricate later.

Diogenes did that to me in the tenth month of his life, gripped by a burst of misplaced affection. And he took me completely by surprise. The result was startling to both of us and ended when I knocked him flying off my shoulder and dropped my favorite pipe on the floor. I believe I also yelled and was quite angry.

Diogenes was—and probably still is—a common crow; not that there was anything in the slightest bit common about him. Indeed, from the moment that I found him huddled miserably on the edge of the highway, a forlorn and emaciated fledgling of ugly mien and nasty disposition, he displayed no common traits whatsoever. He was, in fact, a most intelligent, refined and even sophisticated crow who took an almost immediate liking to me—after he had pecked my hand a few times, that is.

For a while he was too hungry to do more than scream for food and gape his mouth wide every time I came to stuff repulsive subtances down his ever-ready gullet, then to smack his beak in satisfaction. But as he grew—which he did with startling rapidity—he took a few moments after each feeding

to nibble gently on my fingers and to scramble about on my shoulders, now and then tugging at my hair and running a lock or two through his mandibles while making strange noises of love.

He was, despite his affection for me, a tyrant. While he was still fledging he positively demanded food every fifteen minutes, more or less, during the daylight hours and if it was not forthcoming at the first hoarse screams, he would make the house uninhabitable with his yelling. Because of his incessant craving for food, I could not leave him alone in those days and perforce had to tote him wherever I went, sitting like some black, midget potentate in a cardboard box that was lined with plentiful newspaper. And, of course, his jar of mushed-up goo and the glass syringe I used to stuff it down his throat had to come along as well. It was not so bad if I was walking somewhere; Diogenes would swing from my shoulder, his box suspended by a cord, and admire the world about him while digesting his latest repast. But he was a definite nuisance in the car, not only because I had to stop on demand, but because he would insist on getting out of his box and scrambling about upon my person. This not only made driving difficult, but resulted in frequent and liberal staining of the upholstery and my own clothing.

It was a great relief to me when he learned to eat for himself and could strut about inside his roomy cage while I went about my own business. I would often place his cage outside, so he could look about him and importune with his croaks anything living that came within reach of his phenomenally keen eyes. Of course, when I was home, he would not remain in his cage and kicked up such a fuss that I generally gave in to his demands, but by this time he performed his natural functions less frequently, so things were not too bad.

As he grew older and began to fly clumsily around the living room and kitchen, he began getting out of hand. He loved to explore, usually with but one end in sight—to find something to eat—and he would break cups, plates and glasses, knock over the tea and coffee tins, and paddle in the

Common crow

toilet if the bathroom door was open, then scream for me to come and get him out.

The morning he greeted me, as I came downstairs, by landing on my head after a full boisterous flight, I felt it was time for Diogenes to fend for himself. He was big enough, certainly; as the scratches on my head testified, he was equipped with strong claws; and I knew from the worm-in-the-ear episode that there was nothing wrong with his beak or with his aim.

I was fond of him, mind you. He had a happy disposition when he wasn't hungry and he would spend many moments chuckling to himself as he balanced on the back of a kitchen chair and debated his next mischief. But he had to go; I was quite firm about that.

The next morning, I gave Diogenese a feed of all his favorite things: marshmallows, stuffed olives, raisins, peanuts, marmalade on bread, and tomatoes. He gorged and gorged and I believe would have eaten until he dropped dead had I let him. When I stopped, he hopped on my hand and attempted to nibble my nose in gratitude, and the weight of him made me fear that he might never be able to fly again. But not a bit of it!

Outside, and free for the first time since I picked him up off the highway, Diogenes went into a veritable paroxysm of exuberance. He sailed straight up into the air, screaming, then raced off towards the maple woods, stopped halfway to chase a groundhog right up to the door of its burrow, and then disappeared into the green canopy of trees.

Well, that was that, I said to myself. My crow was gone, free, as he had a right and a need to be, and I wouldn't have to put up with his mess and noise ever again. I turned and went into the house and tried to concentrate on the manuscript that I was working on. By lunch time, despite the fact that I had gone outside several times to look for him, there was still no sign of Diogenes. I broke for the noon meal and when I had finished eating I returned to my typewriter and worked steadily all afternoon, reveling in the peace and quiet of a crow-free house.

Just before five o'clock I heard a crow calling. It sounded

The crow is a noisy bird.

too adult and husky for Diogenes so I ignored it, but within a few minutes he landed outside my study window, cawing furiously and tapping at the glass in his efforts to come in. Well, I didn't have the heart to refuse him and, in truth, I was glad to see him, for I had grown almost as attached to him as he had to me. And, I reasoned, I had made considerable gain by getting rid of him for the entire day; now he was just coming home to roost for the night. So I let him in. At once he began screaming for food, getting quite excited and hopping up and down and bowing; then he flew onto my shoulder and nibbled my ear and yelled into it.

I took him downstairs and fed him some of his goodies and banished him to his cage, closing the door firmly. To my surprise, he was quite content to climb on one of his perches and go to sleep, and he stayed that way until five o'clock the next morning, when he woke me up with his hoarse calls. I stumbled down and let him out, whereupon he repeated his previous performance, dashing around madly, cawing and chuckling, and then heading for the maple woods. That night he did not return until dusk.

It took Diogenes four days to learn that he could roost outside just as easily and more comfortably than he could in his indoor cage. It took him another seven days to team up with a roving band of crows and establish himself as a member of the group. Now he would come visiting in the daytime once in a while, to tap on my window and accept some tidbits, then he would fly away again and join his noisy friends and the whole black flock would sail off to find some mischief.

Diogenes left me finally in the fall, heading south with his crow friends, and I have never seen him since. It is winter as I write this chapter, and knowing him, I figure he is probably tapping right now on some window in Florida or Texas, demanding marshmallows and bread and marmalade.

He was an interesting bird and a good friend and he taught me a great deal about crows. Especially did he teach me to respect their intelligence and to admire the determined way in which they go about getting what they want. And, do you know, I believe those black birds can actually count.

Several times, when a few birds were perched in a tree, talking over some matter of great import, they would suddenly give forth a special cry of summons. From all points of the compass the rest of the flock would come, in ones and twos, or more, and land in the meeting tree.

Well, the flock that Diogenes adopted was composed of nineteen birds, including him, and as I watched them organizing their meeting one late afternoon, I wondered how they would know when all the birds in the flock had arrived. I had already noticed that at a certain point they stopped calling and that no more birds flew into the meeting tree after the summons had stopped. So on this occasion I began counting the birds as they arrived. Four of them had begun the summons and the others flew in as usual. When the eighteenth bird arrived I wondered if they would cease calling, for I could see no sign of number nineteen. But no, they continued their cawing, and presently the straggler hove to. Immediately the flock stilled the summons calls.

I watched and counted on numerous occasions after that and the results were always the same. I don't know how they do it, but I am convinced that crows can count!

Monster Bird

Wilshire Boulevard winds its busy course beside the La Brea tar pits in the city of Los Angeles. Thousands of Californians daily stream by in their automobiles; car horns blare, tires squeal. The hectic pace of a modern city ignores the dramas that were once commonplace in and around the black pits that have existed for more than half a million years, holding many of the secrets of prehistoric America. To the average resident of Los Angeles, the La Brea pits are but vague landmarks, not even worthy of a passing glance as a motorist hurries home, but when I first saw them several years ago, the pits exercised a special kind of magic in my mind. Imagination took over and I was transported backwards in time.

It was dawn and the pits lay dormant and dust-covered, death traps for the careless. The fiery redness of an unseen sun highlighted the east and sculpted pink wraiths from rising tendrils of mist. It was the start of a new day during the Pleistocene Epoch, an awakening for the land and for the grotesque creatures that inhabited the region.

Near the edge of one pit lay an inert form. It was partly immersed in the viscous tar, a huge dead creature that had blundered into the quagmire four days earlier. Now it was decomposing, a prehistoric bear slowly sinking into the death hole. The sun tipped above the mountains. The mist wraiths were banished, the land was flooded with sunlight and

California condor

warmth, and thermal updrafts moved in the shimmering air.

From its perch in a tree, a bird flapped its wings. Twelve feet of bone and muscle and feathers fanned the air as *Teratornis* prepared to launch his monster shape into space. The condor shuffled on his perch and put down the ruff of snow-white feathers that had protected his bare neck from the chill of night. He folded his wings, stretched, then took off in flight, knowing that the new-risen sun had increased the thermals sufficiently to carry his weight as he spiraled in search of carrion.

The shadow of the scavenger glided across the land as the bird drifted effortlessly through the air, his orange head with the thunderbird beak moving from side to side in the constant search for death.

Half an hour later *Teratornis* was high over the tar pits and his keen eyes detected the body below. The primitive condor altered his flight pattern, spreading the feathers at the tips of his wings to help him spiral downwards. The whine of air through stiff pinions was clearly audible as the bird dropped.

The treacherous pit looked innocent as the vulture flapped down to land on what he thought was firm footing beside the body of the bear. But in moments the bird was mired by the tar and the more frantic he became, the more tar was smeared on his feathers. *Teratornis* died beside the bear he had come to eat.

By noon, in the fullness of sunshine, the land that was to become California so many thousands of years later basked quietly, all signs of the tragedies it had witnessed sunken into the depth of the pit. There the bones of its victims would rest along with countless others, preserved by the tar, until some half a million years later scientific men would find them, clean them, and learn much about the ancient creatures that roamed and flew in North America's prehistory.

Today it seems likely that *Teratornis*, a bird too big and cumbersome for its own good, slowly modified its shape over the thousands of years that followed its emergence into the North American scene. Eventually the smaller, more streamlined California condor arose to replace *Teratornis*, but today's condor is still large by most standards and it still has some difficulty in launching itself into flight, despite its nine feet of wing span. Seemingly, also, the condor is too large for its environment, for the spectacular vulture is now found only in the mountainous country that lies west of Los Angeles.

In shape and general appearance the condor resembles its remote ancestor, though *Teratornis* seems to have been dark brown with a white ruff, while the modern condor is black with conspicuous white patches under the wings and its ruff is black instead of white. With its orange neck and head and its big wings with their snowy undersides, the condor is a conspicuous bird and easy to identify.

Perhaps because of their great size, condors take a long time to mature after hatching from a pale green or pale blue egg that is about four inches long. Female condors lay only one egg and devote an exceptionally long time to the care of their chick, which may still be fed by the mother when it is fifteen months old. The chick hatches, as a rule, in May and remains in the nest, a great gangling youngster, until about October, when it tries out its wings for the first time and goes for short flights with the parent birds.

Nests may be located in caves high up a mountainside, in hollows among boulders, or even on the ground, in the space between two downed trees, though the birds generally like to nest in high places. The chick is fed by both parents, which regurgitate partly-digested carrion for the youngster.

By the time the young condors learn to fly they are easily as large as their parents, though they lack the white wing patches and they have black heads. But even in this immature plumage they cannot be mistaken for any other North American bird because of their size and the huge wingspan.

Before the American West was settled, condors fed mostly on the carcasses of elk, antelope and deer, picking up dead rabbits and other small animals as they found them. Today, because elk and deer have gone from their range and have been replaced by sheep and cattle, condors feed on the corpses of these domestic animals, many of which die from accidents or disease as they roam through the rangeland.

From studies undertaken by the National Audubon and National Geographic societies, it seems clear that the California condor is not in danger of starving to death and that the birds are continuing to breed normally. But because they do not mate until they are six years old and then breed only every second year, their natural breeding cycle is against them when they are faced by the invasion of their range and by the depredation of thoughtless hunters, who continue to shoot at the slow-flying birds despite the fact that the condor is protected by law.

In the 1960s only some forty condors were thought to remain alive and it seems certain that, despite all the efforts that are being made to preserve this magnificent carrion eater, the relentless march of civilization into the shy bird's domain will eventually lead to its extinction.

The Hoarder

Wherever there is a patch of forest, there is sure to be at least one of the four kinds of nuthatch that live on this continent. Jerking up and down the trees in a constant search for nuts, seeds or insects, these stubby, short-tailed birds are as likely to be seen head downwards as right side up.

These predominantly blue-gray birds always appear to be moving in fits and starts, rather like mechanical toys, but their agility and the ease with which they can walk down any tree-trunk are features that never fail to captivate an observer. They rely upon their long, somewhat curved claws to hold them securely, in whatever direction they may be traveling.

When faced by a nut too large and tough to crack between its jaws, such as a beechnut or an acorn, a nuthatch finds some convenient cranny in the bark of a tree and wedges the nut into it; then it pounds the exposed surface until it cracks the shell and is able to pick out the contents. It is this habit, of course, that has given the bird its name.

Nuthatches are almost constantly employed in the search for food. Much of this they eat on the spot, but they are great hoarders, stuffing nuts and seeds into an endless variety of hiding places. Presumably, this hoarding practice is intended to furnish food "for a rainy day", but it is doubtful whether the birds actually retrieve much of their hidden stores. In the first place, many other birds are well aware of the nuthatch's habits and often follow it around, helping themselves to the goodies as soon as the nuthatch has gone. Squirrels, too, love to raid the bird's stores. And, according to some observers, the nuthatch appears often to forget where it has

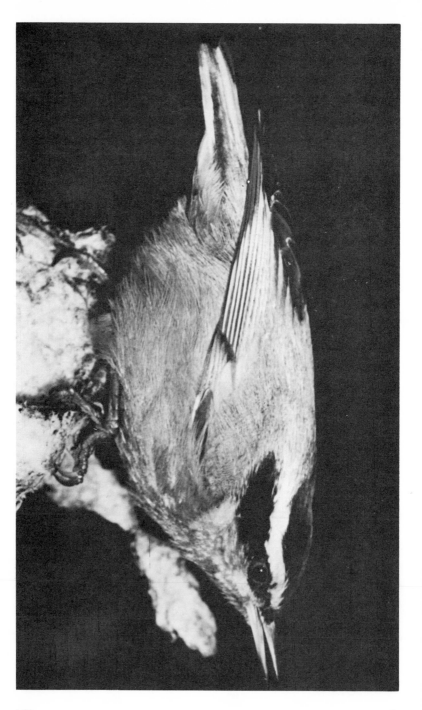

put the food, as it fails to return to it later on.

Hoarding, of course, is a practice indulged in by a large number of birds and by many mammals. It serves, if not always the hoarder himself, at least other species, who benefit from the food, often during hard times. In addition, this hoarding helps to encourage vegetation, when forgotten seeds germinate and grow. No doubt many a tree got its start in this way.

Perhaps the best-known member of the family, because of its wide distribution, is the white-breasted nuthatch, distinguished by its black cap, its white cheeks and underparts, and its larger size. This bird has perhaps the most nasal of all avian accents, uttering an explosive *yank, yank* as it climbs about on trunk or limb or flies through the trees with short, bobbing wing-beats.

Somewhat more northerly in area of distribution, the red-breasted nuthatch is found mainly in coniferous forests, from Alaska to Newfoundland and south in the mountains to southern California and North Carolina. As its name suggests, it has rusty-red underparts; there is also a conspicuous black line running through the eye. It is smaller than the white-breast, measuring between four and five inches.

The brown-headed nuthatch has a chestnut-brown cap, gray back and white underparts. There is a small white patch at the back of its head. It is about the same size as the red-breast, and it lives in pine woods from Oklahoma to Delaware, and south to Florida and the Gulf Coast.

A fourth member of the family, the pygmy nuthatch, which measures usually under four inches, is found in the mountains from southern British Columbia to Arizona and southern California.

Three of the four species of nuthatch spend the winter where they breed, but one, the red-breasted, tends to migrate and may move somewhat south to find balmier weather, ranging as far as the Gulf Coast.

Red-breasted nuthatch

Compulsive Builder

The chipmunk was sitting on a rock near the entrance of her den. Below the ground, in the nesting chamber, her young had been fed and she had come up for a breath of air and a rest from the questing little mouths. She was at peace for a few moments, free of her responsibilities and enjoying the sun on this somewhat chilly day in April.

Suddenly a sprite of a bird, brownish and specked with black and light gray, alighted on a branch of a maple that grew nearby. The house wren was back for another season of nest-building, courting, and feeding on the insects of this piece of mixed forest. The little bird inspected his territory, noted the chipmunk and then voiced his loud, clear, bubbling song, announcing to the world that this was now his home and he would protect it from all members of his species. This done, the wren preened his wings, fussy about his appearance now that he was getting ready to go a-courting.

On her rock, the chipmunk watched the little bird for a moment or two, but she soon lost interest and surrendered herself to enjoyment of the sun, hot on her fur, and of the clear, clean air of the morning. As she sat there, a small ground beetle pushed its way out of a nearby tangle of last year's leaves and began crawling towards a rotting branch, but before it had progressed more than an inch, a small brown bullet of feathers swooped low, pecked once, and the beetle was gone. The wren was down and up in seconds and was voicing his song again before the startled chipmunk had

House wren, with a prize

time to dash for her burrow door. Recognizing the cause of her alarm, she called her displeasure, her soft, husky whistles blending with the blithe song of the wren, who paid no attention to her whatever.

While the two creatures were occupied with the sounds of their own voices, another was watching them. A brown creeper hugged the scaly bark of a red pine with his long claws and studied the scene, examining the ground and the trees and bushes and paying particular attention to the wren, a bird just slightly smaller than himself.

The creeper was already mated and his hen was sitting on five white eggs in a hammock-shaped nest that the two birds had constructed under a piece of loose bark, low down on the trunk of a dead tree. Now the male bird was investigating his territory, checking especially on the newcomer who sang so lustily. For several moments the creeper remained poised against the pine and then, evidently deciding that the wren offered no threat, he opened his long, curved beak and called twice, a high-pitched hissing sound: *seep, seep.*

Instantly the wren stilled his voice and glanced around, a belligerent gleam in his small eyes. The creeper bobbed up the tree with easy grace and the wren at once spotted the movement. The two small brown birds paused to study each other, the stubby, cheeky wren and the slim, quiet creeper who blended almost perfectly with the bark to which he clung. The wren signaled his acceptance by singing melodiously and scanning the ground in the hope of finding another juicy insect; the creeper lisped his small call again and spiraled up the tree, picking at the bark with his thin, curved, needle-sharp beak and swallowing the minute insects that he encountered. When he reached the place where the trunk branched out, he flew down to the base of another tree and started his spiral journey upward once again. Both birds were insect eaters, but each specialized in the manner of his hunting, the creeper being almost exclusively concerned with the tiny organisms that took refuge in the cracks of tree bark, the more active wren taking insects on the wing, from under

Brown creeper

leaves or from the forest floor. The creeper, his beak full of mites and insect eggs, flitted away to deliver the food to his mate.

The wren, his tail held jauntily upright, continued to sing until a passing fly attracted his notice; he flew at it and snapped it up in mid-air. Afterwards he bustled around his chosen territory, inspecting likely nesting sites for an hour or more before he began constructing the first nest. When this was finished to his satisfaction he looked it over and left it, intent on building another home for his prospective mate. This time he chose a small cavity near the chipmunk's burrow, a place where two rocks leaned together to form a dry shelter, with an entrance small enough to admit the wren but not large enough to encourage enemies. Once more the industrious little bird began building, stuffing twigs and grass and old leaves and bits of moss into the cavity.

In the two days that followed, the male built three more nests, each within some form of shelter and each just a little carelessly constructed. Then, on the third day, a female wren arrived. She looked much like the male, though she was slightly smaller, and as she listened to his burst of singing, she seemed to pretend a complete lack of interest. The little male redoubled his efforts. He danced on his perch, puffed out his feathers, held his tail more upright and sang until his whole body shook with the tumbling notes. At last his lady was visibly touched by his efforts. He joined her on her perch and the two sang a duet, her voice every bit as merry and melodious as his. Afterwards he led her away to inspect the nests he had built. And that's when the trouble began!

Female wrens are fussy about their nests and refuse to accept the structures built in their absence. This one settled on the site between the rocks, but she immediately began to pull the nesting material out of the little cave and to scatter it on the ground, much to the dismay of the male. He screamed his anger and danced in rage, fluffing up his feathers and now and then trying to block the entrance to the nesting cavity. But she carried on, determined to have her way, and she pushed past him each time he attempted to stop her. At last he gave up and flew to his favorite perch to vent his frustra-

Wren outside its nesting site

tions. Soon an insect caught his eye; he dived for it, and after he had eaten it he forgot his anger and hunted some more, finding a number of tasty tidbits. When he had satisfied his own hunger he offered his mate a small caterpillar, which she accepted.

When the female finished rebuilding the nest, it was lined with moss and framed with twigs into which she had woven a variety of oddments: bits of bone, small pine cones, stones, the molar of a dead hare, all of which served no particular purpose, neither adding to nor detracting from the utility of the structure. Why did she go to all the trouble to hunt up these strange things and build them into her nest? Who knows?

After the nest was finished, she poked a few small sticks into the entrance of the cavity, to stop other, larger birds from pilfering, and settled to her egg-laying, depositing seven pinkish-white eggs that were liberally sprinkled with reddish dots.

By the time the wren was sitting, the young creepers had hatched and were clamoring for food, and the adults were busy in a constant quest for insects. They patiently hitched their way up the tree-trunks, supporting themselves with their sharp claws and propping their bodies against the tree bark with the stiff feathers on their tails, almost woodpecker-fashion. If they thought danger threatened, each bird would "freeze", its color blending so well with the bark that, on several occasions, a hunting Cooper's hawk sailed close by without seeing them, despite his keen vision. When the threat was gone, the creepers resumed their food hunting and flitted back to their nest with their beaks full of insects.

By late summer, both nests were empty. The young wrens and the young creepers had learned to hunt insects for themselves, each species in its own way. Soon now, the frost would come and the wrens would move a few hundred miles south to avoid the worst of the cold. But the creepers would stay in the forest to face the winter, sustaining themselves on the dormant insects they would painstakingly locate in the trees.

Mournful Pigeon

The mourning dove fluttered down from a nearby tree and walked with purposeful pigeon step towards the pool of water without giving me more than a casual glance. Bobbing its head and treading carefully over the bare rocks that surrounded the small pool, the dove stopped at the water's edge, dipped its beak and began drinking in the distinctive way of all pigeons. Most other birds must get a beakful of water, tip their head back and let the liquid slide down their throat; the members of the pigeon family just suck up their ration of liquid without pausing, as a cow or a horse will do.

This bird I was watching was the male of a pair that was nesting in a locust tree near the house. I had been interested in their doings since they arrived one morning and began their courting rituals outside my bedroom window. It was Sunday morning and I was still in bed, "lying in" at eight o'clock and thinking about a leisurely breakfast before going for a long walk in the spring woods.

The soft, sad cooing of doves disturbed my lazy thoughts and I got out of bed and went to the window. The two birds sitting in the tree had evidently just arrived and were beginning their charming courtship rituals. Every now and then the male bird would fly up 100 feet or more, his body at an angle to the ground, then flap quickly before gliding down in slow, sweeping circles, with stiff wings and spread tail, to land beside the female. On the branch, leaning towards his lady, the dove uttered his soft *ooah, coo, coo, coo,* spreading his tail and showing its black and white fringe. Cooing twice more, he closed his tail feathers. The two birds touched bills

Mourning dove

A soft and gentle bird

for a moment, then the male flew up again, to repeat his courting performance.

Later, he busied himself carrying twigs to his mate, which she fashioned into a rather crude nest that seemed to be too loosely wedged in a fork of a tree. When the two white eggs were laid, both birds shared the task of incubating them, the male sitting during the day and the female taking over from him at evening and warming the eggs until morning.

Despite the proximity of their nest to the house, both birds were trustful and friendly and I was delighted at the chance to watch them from my bedroom window without danger of disturbing them, and perhaps causing them to abandon their eggs. I wondered at first whether my frequent journeys to and from the house would affect them, but they adjusted to me in a surprisingly short time. By the time the eggs were laid and the parents began incubating them, I was sure that they had accepted me completely. Nevertheless, I was always careful to avoid going too close to their tree and I confined my observations to morning and evening watches from the concealment of the window.

On the fourteenth day after incubation began, at nine in the morning, the male bird rose up in the nest and I saw two young pigeons. There was great excitement as the busy parents cared for their young, feeding them at first on "pigeon's milk", a secretion manufactured by the crop, the walls of which thicken to produce this curd-like milky substance. After two days of this special diet, the young were fed on half-digested seeds regurgitated by the parents. They obtained this food by sticking their beaks down the parents' throats.

Like all pigeons, these little ones were not at first pretty. They hunched up their wrinkled bodies and wobbled about whenever they tried to stand. The big heads with their bulbous eyes seemed almost too heavy for the short necks to support. But it was not long before they began to acquire feathers and to take on the sleek, soft look of doves.

Mourning doves are found all over the United States and in southern Canada, in varying numbers according to habitat and food supply. They will nest on the ground where there are no trees.

They are smaller than domestic pigeons, measuring twelve or thirteen inches in length. The tail is long and pointed, rather than fan-shaped as in the pigeon. The buffy-brown head is comparatively small, and is decorated with a single black spot just behind the eye; the back and wings are brown, with a slightly sooty look, but the chest and throat glow with a golden to reddish hue.

Mourning doves often start to breed in February and because of this habit they will raise two, and sometimes as many as three broods each season. They are not particularly numerous, nevertheless, probably because they only raise a maximum of two poults during each hatch.

Unlike the passenger pigeon, which was totally exterminated in the last century by shockingly wasteful hunting and by the clearing of its woodland habitat, most of North America's wild pigeons are relatively safe from the threat of extinction. The mourning dove is still gunned down in some places, principally in the southern States, but it is protected by law in its northern ranges. Many people would wish to see this protection extended to the entire North American continent.

The pair that I was watching raised two broods that year and, when the time came for them to fly southward for the winter, I was indeed sorry to see them go. I was walking back to my home one afternoon when I heard the distinctive, sharp whistling of the wind through their stiff pinions. I looked up and saw a flock of some eighteen doves heading south and as I watched they disappeared over a heavy stand of maple trees that still held some of their glorious red leaves. When I got home, my friendly doves had gone.

Mother Grouse

The air is dry-cold; the snow is white and deep, blanketing the ground and the shrubs and the small trees, and hanging in sculpted forms on the branches of the evergreens. The deciduous trees stand stark, their shadows forming black tracings on the snow. The rays of the morning sun slant down from a clear blue sky and are scattered into rainbow hues by a million minute snow crystals.

There is a hill. Beneath its topping of snow, mosses and small plants are sheltered from the cold; they are anchored in a thin layer of brown soil that covers the ancient rock of the pre-Cambrian shield. On the leeward side of the hill stands a thick cluster of balsam firs: young trees, deep-skirted, bearing a heavy layer of snow that the winds have been unable to carry away. In a small open space within the shelter of the balsams a hole has been punched in the snow. It is some seven inches long by five inches wide and issuing from it are three-toed tracks that lead to the base of the largest tree on the knoll.

It is the trail of the hen grouse and the hole is where she sheltered last night, seeking the insulation of snow to avoid the thirty-below-zero temperature that gripped the forest. Now she is foraging, stepping slowly and carefully through the balsam's branchy skirts, picking up old partridge berries, a dormant insect here and there, the fall buds of some young poplar trees. As she breakfasts, she calls softly, a high, peeping sound that carries down the hill and is echoed by two more grouse that are likewise seeking food this morning.

Yesterday the hen almost died. Today it is as though the

danger of last evening had never existed, as though the flashing teeth of the coyote had not grazed her tail, plucking from it one of the broad feathers, the jerk caused by the pulling teeth rocking her off her flight course and almost causing her to collide with the trunk of a large poplar. Forget the danger that is passed, urges the wilderness to all her creatures; do not dwell on fear, but remember instead the lessons of survival. The grouse obeyed and was now intent on food, a dominant need in face of the bitter cold. But she was not careless. She knew the dangers of the forest and she watched and listened for them as she moved quietly, supported on the soft snow by the comb-like projections that now fringed her toes, but that would fall away in spring.

There are timber wolves here, and coyotes and foxes and bobcats, meat prowlers by day or night. And there are owls: the great horned owl, "tiger" of the dark; the snowy owl that hunts as often by day as by night. So while the hen eats, she is vigilant, and her soft calls, which might seem to be a giveaway of her position, are in reality an added precaution, for they elicit response from the other hens, assuring her that there is no cause for alarm. They serve another purpose, also, offering distraction to a predator, who hears three or four calls coming from different places and may spend precious moments making up his mind which bird to attack, heartbeats of time that may allow one of the grouse to spot the hunter and raise the alarm.

It had been like that yesterday. The hen was soft-stepping over the snow, seeking a refuge for the night, and her companions were busy on similar quests, each bird calling in its high voice. The coyote had smelled them some time earlier and had stalked them carefully, using cover to get closer, keeping himself low to the ground, for he well knew the keenness of sight and hearing possessed by these wild fowl.

When he was close enough for a rush, but still not close enough to see the birds among the low-hanging balsam boughs, the calls distracted him. He could not decide which way to run as, first from one side then from another, the quiet

Ruffed grouse chick

calls reached him. So he had stretched upwards with shoulders and neck, trying to catch sight of one of the birds. Instead it was the hunter who was seen, and immediately the alarm call was sounded. In almost perfect unison five woodsy-brown bodies hurtled up from the ground with a loud whir of wings, into the shelter of the higher tree branches. The hen had been closest to the small wolf and he had charged her, leaping mightily, stretching his lean body to its utmost, and almost succeeding in reaching her. But when he landed heavily and awkwardly in the snow, his only reward had been a tail feather, and he had wandered away, seeking other prey.

This had not been a new experience for the hen. She had been subjected to numerous attacks from coyotes and owls and bobcats, and once a timber wolf had almost caught her, but she had learned from each encounter. She had survived five winters in the northwoods. And she had mated four times and hatched her young during four springs.

Now her main concern was survival, finding sufficient food to keep her body warm in the harsh winter, and escaping the clutches of predators who were likewise driven by hunger. Her experience and her health were allies that promised to keep her alive long enough to produce another clutch of downy chicks. So the hen fed this morning, watchful yet unafraid.

Now spring is in the north woods. The snow has gone, the ground is responding to the urge of warm winds and moisture and to the energy of sunlight. On the hilltop, small fungi grow amid the moss, wintergreen sends up its snowy flowers, blueberries are beginning to bud. Insects move; small birds. arrive from the south. The drumming of a ruffed grouse cock fills the wilderness with its staccato, engine-like sound.

Strutting puffed up on a downed long, the cock beats his wings: *bup, bup, bup, bup-bup-bup-bupbupbupbup*. . . . As the speed of the beating wings displaces air, the booming is like the sound of muffled drums. The cock pauses, then fans out his black-banded tail once more, erects his brown ruff and his

Ruffed grouse

sharp crest, and struts, picking up one foot almost mechanically, setting it down on the log, picking up the other foot. Once again, he beats his wings in courtship ardor.

Watching him from a perch on the lower branches of a young balsam, the hen waits for his attentions. She must not interrupt this ceremony; she knows that if she approaches her lord just now he will probably chase her away, not wishing to be disturbed during this supreme moment of his life. So the hen waits, knowing that soon she will get his attention.

The sun rises higher in the sky, and as its light shines through the balsam needles the hen notices a stout, black ground beetle as it scurries through the mulch on the forest floor. Quickly she hops down from her perch and grasps the beetle, swallowing it. Her movement captures the cock's notice. The male puffs his soft brown, white and bluish-black feathers as he prepares to make one more drum-roll before advancing on the hen. Again his wings fan air and the sound of his mating call fills the woods. When his wings are still and drooping at his sides, he hops off the log and walks towards the waiting hen.

A month has now passed and the hen is sitting on her clutch of eggs. There are eleven buffy eggs in the nest that she has fashioned out of leaves and a few feathers, in a hollow under a downed tree. Bird and nest blend so well with the woodland background that they are almost impossible to detect. The hen sits immobile, relying on stillness and camouflage for protection.

Two days earlier a prowling fox had passed within five feet of the nest without noticing the statue-like bird. A week before that a bobcat had winded her and she had left the nest, sliding off the cup and stepping quietly away from it until she was about ten yards from her eggs; then she began calling loudly, with sounds of distress, and she flopped on the ground as though severely injured. The big hunting cat had crouched and stalked her and she had led him away from her nest, now getting up and running a few yards, now dropping down and pretending injury. As soon as she had led the bob-

Grouse returning to the nest

cat far enough from her eggs to ensure their security, she rose on sturdy wings and beat away, deep into the bush. Perched on a spruce bough, she listened to the cat's progress and noted that he was heading away from her nest. Then she flew back and continued brooding her eggs.

While she sat there, her mate, the boisterous cock bird, was foraging through the woods, unburdened by the cares of parenthood. His duty to life was behind him, his drumming days were over for another year, and if he and the other cockbirds attracted predators away from the sitting hens, they did so unwittingly.

Twenty-four days have passed since the hen began to sit. It is morning. Under the warm softness of the hen's feathers one of the bantam-size eggs begins to crack as the chick within uses his tiny egg-tooth, located on the tip of his upper beak, to break through the shell. The hen clucks quietly, knowing that her chicks are ready to emerge; she moves, lifting one wing and peering down, and she shuffles her body, turning some of the eggs. One by one the chicks break out. They are soaked by the moisture that was contained within the egg, but they are active and begin to call with their small voices even before they have broken completely away from the shell. An hour later ten chicks nestle under the hen. Now they are dry and they are strong and active. By mid-afternoon the hen leaves the nest and takes her brood with her. They are safer loose in the forest, where, upon hearing their mother's alarm call, they will quickly scatter to crouch down and become invisible while she leads the threat in another direction. One egg remains in the nest; she knows it will never hatch.

Within the sunlight and shadow of their home range, the chicks blend completely into their surroundings. They are colored like the forest floor, light yellow dappled with varying shades of brown. Downy and small though they are, they can run swiftly and quietly and have an instinctive knowledge of the use of camouflage.

As the weeks pass and the chicks grow, they begin to acquire their adult plumage and by the end of the summer they can fly almost as well as their mother and are able to take care of themselves. Still, the mother leads them and tries to protect them for a little while longer. Three of her brood have fallen prey to the hunters. One was killed by a weasel, another was picked up by a red-tailed hawk, yet another became a meal for a fox.

And now autumn has come to the northwoods. The young grouse are on their own. Almost as large as their mother, they scurry and fly through the forest, scurfing up the ground with their well-clawed feet in search of insects, feasting on partridge berries and on tree buds, on scarlet wintergreen berries and on almost all the kinds of vegetation offered by the wilderness. There is no shortage of food and the grouse put on weight and build up the all-important fat that will help them survive the rigors of the northland's cold.

The Orphan

The summer storm had been severe, with lashing rain, strong winds and much thunder and lightning. But, as is so often the case, the furious elements quickly relented and the humid earth was steaming under the hot June sun as I went for my afternoon walk. It was Saturday, and on the Monday I was due to drive to Ottawa to speak to a number of librarians at a conference there. My thoughts were on this task as I walked near a large beaver pond and I had actually stepped over the poplar branch before my brain registered what I had seen.

The branch had been broken off by the storm, to judge by the freshness of its leaves and the whiteness of the scar on the parent tree. It was a stout limb, about three inches in diameter where it had joined the trunk. Two-thirds of the way along its length was the basket nest of a Baltimore oriole. I bent down to examine the nest. In it were four white eggs, traced with brown, and one baby oriole, a new hatchling. It was still wet from its birth and a bit of the egg-shell was sticking to its back. What should I do? The little bird was alive, and comfortable enough inside the beautifully-woven nest, but I was sure it was doomed.

Being aware of the very fragile balance that often exists in a wild environment, I do not, as a rule, interfere with nests or young birds, limiting myself to long-range observations through field glasses and rescuing young ones only in dire emergencies. But this *was* an emergency. The mother might return and try to raise it there on the ground, but I knew the chances of this were slim. I knew also that the young bird would not last long, unprotected in its fallen nest, for if the

cold did not kill it, almost certainly some predator would. Still, I waited a couple of hours before picking up nest, baby and eggs and carrying them away. And during my wait, sitting quietly under a large tree, I saw no sign of the adult oriole.

At home I fed the little one with an eyedropper. I knew I had undertaken a formidable task if I was to raise it. Young birds must be fed at very frequent intervals during the daylight hours and this becomes a real chore for the well-meaning human who would act as foster parent.

I spent the remainder of that Saturday and all day Sunday pouring various mixtures into the little bird, feeding it a balanced ration that contained such things as vitamins in tiny doses, chopped egg yolk, bits of finely-strung meat and other delicacies that required a fair amount of preparation. I did little else, in fact, but care for the youngster and it was not until Sunday evening that I realized that I would have to take it with me to Ottawa!

The trip from my farm home to Canada's capital normally took six hours to drive, but that Monday it took me eight, for I had to stop at frequent intervals to feed my ever-hungry charge. By this time the little bird had fully accepted me as its parent; I had only to touch the nest in which it was still housed and it would gape profusely and utter its reedy little hunger cry.

In Ottawa, I explained my predicament to the officials who were waiting for me—I was late arriving that evening, of course—and I smuggled the oriole and its nest into my hotel bedroom. Then I went off to dinner. In the course of this official function, I had to make many exits, popping in and out of the dining room in order to feed the oriole. It became too much for one of my table companions, who, halfway through the meal, leaned over to enquire if I was unwell!

The next day, during a cocktail hour in my host's suite with some eight or nine librarians, I felt I had to explain about my ward. Once the initial surprise was over, all of those people wanted to see the little bird and I went to col-

The wonderful nest of the oriole

lect it. The rest of that hour was devoted to the oriole and the reason for our meeting was quite forgotten.

The little bird thrived and grew larger and more demanding, and the cares of parenthood were heavy upon me. Each time it defecated—which was usually after each meal—it was necessary to clean out the mess. Nature invented the plastic garbage bag long before man, so that small birds usually deposit their litter neatly wrapped in a little bag that the mother bird picks up and tosses out of the nest. But I was not quite as adept as a female oriole in this task and the tweezers I used for this purpose often punctured the bag. As a result, the nest was soon too soiled for the little bird and I then placed it in a cardboard box that I lined often with fresh tissue.

The fledgling grew stronger and began to explore, and one day I arrived in the kitchen to find the nesting-box empty. After some searching, I located the oriole under the chesterfield, from where I coaxed it with the eyedropper. Now that the youngster could fly, I had to cage it. I fed it less often and tried to ignore its constant demands, in order to encourage it to peck for itself.

At last my task was done; the young bird was fully fledged and it could fly and feed itself. With a mixture of sadness and elation I released it. For a few days it stayed around the house and would fly to me when I went outside, posturing with its wings and demanding food; then it left and I saw it no more.

Orioles belong to the same family as meadowlarks and blackbirds and, like their relatives, are widespread on the North American continent. Several species of oriole live in Canada and the United States, of which the Baltimore oriole and its western counterpart, the Bullock's, are perhaps the best known. Recently, because these two forms interbreed where their ranges overlap, the American Ornithological Union has decided that they should be classed as one species— the northern oriole.

The male northern oriole, resplendent in breeding plumage

of orange, black and white, is a magnificent fellow indeed, and his mate is no less beautiful in her similar, but somewhat paler garb.

The orchard oriole is of more southerly distribution, nesting throughout the eastern United States, but in only a few localities in Canada. The male is handsome, clad in rich chestnut on chest and back, where the northern oriole is orange. The female, however, is a drab greenish-brown.

Like the meadowlarks and blackbirds, the orioles are sweet singers, voicing their rich, piping melodies as soon as they arrive in their nesting areas. Their song is variable and each bird appears to render stanzas of its own composition.

As a nest builder, the female oriole has no peer. Hanging upside down, she constructs a framework of plant fibers, dangling from the branchlets of a tree, as high as sixty feet from the ground; then she weaves an exquisite purse-shaped nest, some six inches deep, using plant fibers, hair, yarn, string or any other likely material. Within this fine basket she lays her eggs.

Birds of Confusion

The identification of birds in their natural habitat has attracted millions of enthusiasts from all over North America.
Those who have not yet succumbed to this fascinating hobby
may wonder what attracts so many men, women and children
to the art—for an art it really is! There are, of course, many
pleasant experiences to be gained from bird watching, even if
not a single bird is seen—a rather unusual, but still possible
event—and not the least of these is the effect upon the watcher of the outdoors itself. No one would deny the pleasures of
the woods in summer, or the beauty of walking through an
open meadow, by the edge of a lake or river, or along the
seashore. But many people do not fully appreciate the peace
to be found and the number of birds to be seen in our city
gardens, parks and ravines.

Yet, as any bird watcher will testify, there is more to the
"game" than the pleasures of forest and lake, or the lure of
the outdoors; there is a challenge that few can resist once
they have tried it. There are, in fact, several challenges. To
begin with, although the forest may be full of birds, seeing
any one of them clearly enough to allow for positive identification is often hard to do. You sit on a log or stand under a
tree, field glasses ready, and you hear the singing of a nearby
bird. "It must be in *that* tree," you say to yourself or to your
companion, as you raise the glasses to your eyes and twiddle
the focus wheel. A wall of green enters your vision, fuzzy at
first, like a badly-tuned television picture, then clearer, so that

Yellow warbler

each leaf and branch stands out. Perhaps you also see a number of insects and patches of blue sky—but no bird. After a time, glasses are lowered and eyes search the canopy of green.

Suddenly a brightly-colored flash appears from behind some leaves; a bird, but what kind? It teases the watcher with a glimpse of body and wings, then it darts into another cluster of leaves. The glasses come up again, but while one is lifting them the bird has darted away in a new direction.

At last the songster is still long enough for a clear view. Five seconds, ten, fifteen go by and you note color, size, shape. Just as you have observed all these things, the bird flits away, back into the forest. Even if you happen to know the bird already and have made a positive identification, you are left with a slightly cheated feeling. You wanted to look at it for a few moments longer, to take pleasure from its delicate colors and from its actions. Oh well, maybe next time. . . . But if you are a beginner, you sometimes verge on despair. You needed just one more look to be *sure*.

Many birds pose these challenges to the watcher, but none more than the wood warblers, a large family of chiefly insect-eating birds that are found only in the western hemisphere. There are over 100 different species of wood warblers, and of these some fifty-seven are found on our northern continent.

For the beginning bird watcher, the very thought of distinguishing fifty-seven species of one family would be confusing enough. Not only are most of them similar in size, and many in color, but to add to this confusion is the fact that most of these birds change their plumage pattern twice a year. They appear in the spring in their courting colors, then, as the summer progresses, gradually assume an often quite different fall plumage. As if this were not enough, adult females usually differ from the males during the breeding season, while young just out of the nest and immature birds are different again.

This means that amateur enthusiasts—and even seasoned watchers—must learn to identify a particular species in as many as four plumages, so that the next time a female of a

Unlike most warblers, the ovenbird nests on the ground.

species pops into focus, or a male, or an autumnal young bird, or a fledgling, they will remember the change of garb and recognize the bird for what it is. Quite a chore! Quite a challenge! And an art that is capable of instilling deep satisfaction each time one learns to recognize a previously unfamiliar species.

But take heart. Warblers live in various habitats and in various geographical locations. Each species has a different song. Learn about these things, and you are half way to beating the challenges of warbler watching, which is one of the more difficult yet fascinating aspects of the art of "birding".

As a class, warblers are small, slim birds—five inches or so in length—and are often brightly colored. With their slender, pointed beaks, they skillfully gather a wide variety of insects, which constitute the major part of their diet. Habitually, most of their foraging is done in the woodlands, some species haunting willow thickets or the alders bordering a lake, others staying in the high tree-tops. Some like to hunt in the broadleaved trees, while others prefer the evergreens.

Because their prey moves quickly, warblers are ever on the go. They fly rapidly from branch to branch, in pursuit of a luscious insect, then another, then one more. Then, beak full, they zip away to the nest to feed their gaping young ones.

The very name applied to this family of small birds is misleading, for our North American warblers do not really warble! They sing, of course, with great abandon, but their voices are not particularly musical (with some exceptions), for which they would seem to try to compensate by putting plenty of energy and variety into their songs. The songs of the warblers are distinctive enough, however, to be useful for purposes of identification—once you have learned them, that is!

There is hardly a region of North America that does not have its share of these spritely little birds. The magnificent red-faced warbler, a bird that is like fire, smoke and charcoal in its plumage, is found in Arizona and New Mexico. The blackburnian warbler, the male of which is black and white, bedecked with glowing orange on the breast, neck and head, breeds from the midwest to the east of the northern United States and southern Canada. From Nebraska to Rhode Island and south to Texas and Florida, the hooded warbler sings *please to, pleased to meet you* as it flies through its patch of forest, flashing its black cowl and its yellow face and underparts. From Minnesota to New York and New Jersey, south to Texas, Florida and the Gulf, the rich yellow head and breast of the prothonotary warbler are a delight to spot. In the northernmost forests of Canada, the blackpoll warbler raises its brood and then turns around and flies all the way to South America, the little black-and-white-striped bird with the black cap holding the record for making the longest migration flight of any songbird.

So they go, these strictly North American birds, heading north in spring and turning southward again in the fall, eating vast quantities of insects and giving endless hours of pleasure to those who devote themselves to their study. Our forests would not be the same without the cheerful presence of these beautiful little birds.

ready become accustomed to the blind and to my comings and goings. Every now and then the whiskered face of a beaver will pop up, observe the blind and the human, and move slowly in a wide circle before disappearing into an area of reeds and water lilies.

Now we must leave the campsite and go to the island, paddling slowly and quietly in the canoe that is drawn up ready at the lake edge. On reaching the island, we shall take our places within the sackcloth shelter, for soon the bustle of bird life will reach its peak. Already the voices of the birds are filling the air around us, as we head for the blind: red-wings and grackles, jays and chickadees, marsh wrens and crows, ducks and herons and bitterns and a host of others. Far away, on the mainland, a wood thrush sings his bell-like phrases, and on the lake a loon spills its laughter.

As we enter the blind, the birds pour their songs upon the dawn, some melodious, others harsh, some shy and whispered. The slight, pungent smell of sackcloth mixes with the sharp smell of the repellent we have sprayed upon ourselves, and these scents mix with the odors of the lake. In a few moments we shall become accustomed to these things; now they are strong in our nostrils, though not unpleasant, and they remind us of the quest that we have undertaken here. We sit silently in the blind, peering through the holes in its walls, watching the lake, while we clutch notepad and pencil and make ready to scribble the names of the creatures that we see, to record some of their behavior. . . .

The sky, we note, is reflected on water that is almost totally still, the surface disturbed only by gentle ripples as unseen life and currents activate the lower levels of the lake.

Suddenly the placid water opposite the western-facing window of the blind begins to erupt, rolling upwards sluggishly to form a liquid mound. This is almost at once replaced by the head and body of a smallish, chunky water bird that wears a conspicuous golden "horn" on each side of its head.

Horned grebe

Between these feathered tufts, the head and cheeks of the bird are jet black; on its back, the dark feathers shine deep blue. A wide band of rufous begins at the erect neck and extends down the flanks. As the duck-like creature raises itself slightly in the water, we see its white breast. "Horned grebe," we write; then, as five brownish-striped young ones scuttle quickly into view, we note further, "female with young."

The mother grebe drops something on the surface of the water and her fuzzy youngsters dash to it, each anxious for a share of the morsel that we can't quite recognize; it may be a leech, or a small fish, or a water beetle. The scramble ends. One chick holds his head up and his throat muscles work as he swallows his prize. The mother bobs her body once, then dives suddenly, cleaving the water as she streaks downward to seek more food for her young. The babies swim about aimlessly, waiting for the return of their mother.

The young grebes look to be about three weeks old, which means that the eggs from which they emerged were laid some seven weeks ago, for the young hatch in twenty-four or twenty-five days. But before the eggs could be laid, the courting ritual had to take place, as the male and female indulged in their complex nuptial dances. The birds trod water with their unwebbed feet and rose upright to face one another; then they circled, face to face, shaking their golden plumes and now and then touching beaks. Then came the mating, and the egg-laying in the untidy floating nest that was anchored to the growing cat-tails. Both birds shared the task of incubation, taking turn and turn about.

After the young were born, father and mother escorted their precocious brood, taking them among the cat-tails for shelter, herding the quick-moving babies away from danger, or keeping a sharp watch while the young grebes swam carelessly on open water. Then, as the babies grew stronger and were better able to take care of themselves, the male grebe seemed to tire of parental duties. Gradually he moved away, each morning exploring a little farther from the nesting area

---

The grebe wears ear-tufts only during the breeding season.

Horns of Gold

My tent nestles under the shade of a big balsam fir and my
camp overlooks a wilderness lake. My days are highlighted by
the voices and the colors of the birds, by the bustle of their
lives as they feed and build their nests and raise their young.
I am here to watch, to photograph as many as I can, to observe their actions; to catalogue the species as I find them.
How many different kinds of birds live in the area of this
northern Ontario lake? What do they eat? Where do they
build their nests? I am trying to discover some of these things
and to record my findings. You, the reader, may join me;
you may come and spend a few days with me beside this
lake, which, though it happens to be in Ontario, is yet repre-
sentative of the habitat frequented by many of the birds of
North America. We could just as easily visit some secluded
place in Minnesota or Ohio, Quebec or Alberta. But this is
an area I know well, a place in which I have spent many seasons. It is my "neighborhood", just as the street and district
in which city people dwell become their own special domain.

Dawn, July 1st. In the east, the rosy light of day creeps
into the pale sky, rimming the distant trees and highlighting
their shapes. On the wild grasses and shrubs there is dew,
fresh and crystalline, spreading a sheen on blades and leaves
and hanging in little globules on the tips of small plants.
I have set up my bird blind on a small rock island in the
center of the small lake. Almost beneath it, at the water's
edge, sits an untidy beaver lodge, whose occupants have al-

and staying away longer. At last he stayed away altogether and the mother continued to take care of her young, alone.

This morning she is teaching them how to hunt, now and then breaking off her instruction to dive deeply and find some succulent bit of life. Often she shares it with the brood, for the undisciplined youngsters scare away more food than they can catch and the surface hunting has not been good this day. The young circle expectantly around another one of those gentle upheavals of water made by the rising bird. The mother appears, holding a large tadpole between her pointed mandibles; it is the tadpole of a bullfrog, still wriggling feebly, a creature about two inches long with a fat, round body and a tapering tail. The mother drops it on the water. Again there is a scramble and the water boils as the little grebes seek to gain the food. One succeeds and pulls out of the melée, swallowing frantically.

Suddenly the mother bird looks up, uneasy about something. She remains still on the water and one of her youngsters climbs on her back and disappears into the feathered "pocket" between her wings. The mother grebe lets loose an ear-splitting screech, her cry of alarm. At once the water boils as the family race for shelter in the cat-tails.

The Harrier

Coming in swiftly from the northern end of the lake, on long, narrow wings, a large hawk quests for prey. He sees the grebes, but is too far away to drop on one of the young ones. He keeps coming, gliding above the tops of the cat-tails, holding his wings above the horizontal.

The blue-gray head and back are visible as the bird passes the blind, and when he veers swiftly to investigate something among the lily pads we see his large white rump-patch. He is about eighteen inches long and has a wingspan about equal to his length. His extended wings display black edgings. "Marsh hawk, male," we note, as we watch.

The hawk turns once more and glides past the blind, then he disappears among the shrubs and willows that border the shoreline to the southeast, still skimming low, keen eyes searching and quick ears listening for the stir or rustle of mouse, mole, or duckling. The grebes watch him, from the safety of the cat-tails.

A quarter of a mile away, concealed by the thick shelter of a dwarf juniper bush, the big female, brown where her mate is gray, on the upper parts of the body, guards the five white-downy young and waits for her mate to return with food. Three days ago we visited this nest and watched the female and her young; she did not take great fright at our presence, and was content to mantle her brood with her wings, provided we kept our distance.

The two hawks were born on this lake several years ago

and each of them was marked by me, while in its own nest. They still wear the conspicuous orange rings that I fastened around their ankles and that are easily visible with glasses. The male, and the other young that were in his nest, I banded on the right leg; those in the female's nest, I banded on the left. The experiment was undertaken to establish some of the habits of these birds. Of the seven young marsh hawks that I banded, only these two returned to the area of the lake, and it was with excitement that I observed their courtship ceremonies.

This year they returned again, and I watched them as the male began his spectacular nuptial dives. Rising sixty feet or more above the trees, the hawk would suddenly halt in midair for a fraction of time, then launch his body towards the ground, screaming shrilly. Down, down, down he plunged, as though he would never stop. But seconds before the graceful bird smashed into the ground, a quick movement of the tail, a checking with the wings, and he pulled out with ease, to begin climbing the sky anew. Again and again he repeated these maneuvers, tirelessly, effortlessly, while his brown mate watched him from a hummock in the low meadow.

Now and then, the female would join him in the air and the two would indulge in a brief display of aerobatics, then she would return to the area that she had already chosen for her nest. He, indefatigable, continued to dive and climb, plummeting his sturdy body towards the ground seventy or more times before he at last broke off to go hunting with his mate.

After this show-off time, the pair settled to the serious task of raising one more brood of marsh hawks. The male busied himself gathering nesting materials to take to his mate; she fashioned these into the cup of the nest, first making a crude platform on the ground, within the shelter of the juniper.

When the nest was done, the female laid four eggs, blue and white and faintly splotched with brown, one each day. Now both birds took turns sitting and warming the eggs, turning them at regular intervals, so that the developing

---

Male marsh hawk at the nest

embryos would not become stuck to the insides of the shells.

Four weeks later, the young hawks chipped themselves free of their shells. They were feeble, naked little creatures, who tottered about the nest and thrust their ugly heads through the mother's feathers. As the days passed, they grew woolly down on their bodies and their ungainly heads began to acquire the austere but aristocratic mien of their parents.

The mother hawk still remained close to her young, but now and then she would take off on short hunting trips, helping her mate in his constant search for food. While the parent birds were on these forays, the young would scramble about in the nest, still unsteady, occasionally tripping each other and falling. One fell out of the nest, struggled to its feet and tried to return, only to move farther away from its shelter of green.

Emerging into the open, the young hawk shrilled its fear, and its calls immediately alerted a sinuous brown animal that was moving through the underbrush. The weasel pointed himself towards the young hawk, its cry of distress telling him that here was food for the taking. In seconds, the quick, sharp fangs bit deep, and the young hawk died. The weasel dragged the body away, disappearing with it into the shrubs just as the female hawk returned. If she noticed the disappearance of one of her brood, she gave no sign. She was carrying a chipmunk and she ripped its body and fed her young.

An hour later, the insatiable weasel returned to the nest. He had eaten the young hawk, but the fast pace of his life gave this small predator an enormous hunger. He came in the hope of finding another meal. Instead, he found death.

The female hawk heard his rustlings through the grass and she jumped off the edge of her nest and took to her wings. In moments she had located the weasel. He sought escape, but the hawk pounced, her long legs, with their needle-sharp talons, stretching ahead of her body as she clutched the weasel and set her claws. In an instant it was done. The fierce little hunter would hunt no more.

The appearance of the weasel has disturbed the female

hawk and she has stayed near her nest for some days. Her mate now hunts alone for himself and his family, flapping and gliding as he systematically quarters his territory. At sight of prey, the long tail slams down suddenly, arresting the bird's progress, and the hawk drops in his killing stoop, eyes fixed firmly on his prey. Comes the kill, legs outstretched, claws reaching, digging in, then he is off the ground once more, whistling shrilly, his prey gripped in one foot.

The hawk flies higher, angling towards the nest, and the female sees him. She rises from the nest and as she gains height the male releases his prey. The female flies in, grasps the food in mid-air and carries it to her young. The male sets off on another hunt, flying into our field of vision, directly towards the blind. We watch, spellbound, as he swoops past the blind and disappears into the willow patch. In another moment he comes back into view, flying right past our blind and level with it, and we clearly see the muskrat that dangles from his talons, two streaks of blood, twin lines of red, etching the dark brown fur.

The Shy One

An hour has passed, and the area we are watching has remained empty of birds. The lake is still and quiet. A lilac-blue damselfly flits past the blind on wings of lace, hovers right in front of our eyes for a moment and then swiftly captures a mosquito. Beside the rocky island upon which we perch, the water-lily leaves become resting places for frogs and water insects.

The sun is high and hot, burning into us through the sack-cloth, so that our bodies trickle with moisture. But, uncomfortable as we are, the heat of the day brings its own blessing: it has chased most of the bloodsucking insects to shelter on the undersides of leaves and on grass stems, and for this we are glad.

The noonday hush has settled over the lake and the forest. We know that most of the birds will remain secluded and silent during the heat of the day, and that our chances of a sighting are poor. But we decide to wait a little longer, hoping to see just one more bird before we desert the blind for our own midday siesta. So we draw on our stock of patience and we continue our vigil, itching a little from the fly bites and wiping our glistening faces now and then. Sooner or later, some bird will come.

At last we note movement on the west bank of the lake. A greenish-black, crow-sized bird is emerging from the bushes

Green heron

with great stealth and slowness, its long legs stilting carefully.

"Green heron," we enter into the log. Then we settle to watch a bird that is not often seen in the open like this. The green heron is a retiring creature, always alert and ever ready to freeze into immobility or to scuttle out of sight into the alder thickets. Then, too, this lake is slightly north of its usual range; I have seen a green heron in this area only twice before.

We notice that the heron's dark back and wings are glossy, their sheen changing from green to green-black to green-blue as the light strikes them. We admire the bird's chestnut cheeks and neck, and its white throat and neck-stripe. Its underparts are dark bluish-gray, setting off the orange legs.

The heron nears the water and pauses at its edge, scanning the area. It pays special attention to an old log that lies partly submerged, the lower end buried in the mud, the higher end projecting above the water. The heron takes two steps forward into the shallow water, and hops up on the log. Now another pause to look around and, evidently satisfied, it walks up its perch to the highest point, where it stands, still as a statue, with head tilted down and long, sharp beak ready for instant action.

We watch carefully, for this bird is obviously hungry and we may be privileged to see the manner in which it hunts. Five minutes slip by, then ten; the little heron has not moved. Two or three more minutes pass, and then we see that the bird has become tense. It has not really moved, but the toes are clenched tighter on the log and there is a new rigidity in its posture.

Suddenly, the heron pivots forward and down, stabbing with its beak while the toes anchor themselves on the wooden perch, almost as though the bird was hinged to the log by its feet. In a moment, the head lifts out of the water, dripping, with a large bullfrog secure between its mandibles. The heron regains its balance on the log, raises its head and swallows the frog. Afterwards, it becomes a statue again and another ten minutes go by before it once more lunges at the water.

This time it captures a catfish. Instead of swallowing it right away, it flips the fish into the air, catches it headfirst, then swallows. Instinctively, it knows the difference between the frog, with its round, dull bones, and the fish, with its backward-sloping spinees and sharp fins that would be a hindrance if it were swallowed tailfirst.

The green heron appears satisfied. It yawns, a rather comical gesture to those of us watching, for as the thin mandibles open wide they give the bird a startled look. After the yawn, the heron launches itself off the log, flapping lazily away, stilty legs held backwards.

Once (and only once!), I surprised a green heron as it perched on a branch of a small alder near a marsh. I had been following a game trail which bordered the wetlands and the ground underfoot was carpeted with moss, which made walking almost totally silent. The wind was blowing towards me, and for a moment the heron, evidently intent on something in the marsh, was not aware of my presence. As I turned a bend in the trail, there it was, broadside to me. What a chance for a picture! As quietly as possible, I tried to get my camera trained on the bird, but it spotted my movement. Startled, it raised its crest and flew away, yelling its alarm, a two-syllabled, rather staccato call that sounded like this: *skee-ow!*

Masters of Flight

After the green heron has gone, we drink coffee, but discard the sandwiches, which have gone stale in the heat. As we sip, we watch. There is a beaver swimming in leisurely manner towards the lodge above which we sit. It has lost all fear of our blind. A school of minnows suddenly erupts out of the water, perhaps chased by a larger fish. The calls of birds reach us now and then, particularly the blue jays, which are screaming one moment and mimicking the next, making blue flashes of color that we can see occasionally through the trees on the shore. A red squirrel chatters somewhere nearby; we can't see him, but we know that some intruder has dared to enter his domain and the little rodent is roundly cursing. Presently we hear the voice of a marsh wren and we notice the tips of some cat-tails moving slightly as the small, brown bird forages for insects, but it remains concealed, so we cannot enter it into our log.

Now the coffee is drained and it is getting too hot to linger in the blind. So we leave the steaming shelter and scramble gratefully into the canoe, paddling to our landing site across the water in but five minutes.

As we brush against the foliage on shore, we disturb small clouds of mosquitoes, that fly up to seek our blood, attracted by the heat of our bodies and, some scientists believe, by the carbon dioxide that we exhale. I, too, share this view. Once I took a sort of self-administered "breathalyzer test" by blowing up a large balloon, in which I had first pierced a tiny

Turkey vulture in glorious flight

hole, and hanging it outside to see if my slow-leaking breath, high in carbon dioxide, would attract the mosquitoes. The balloon took nine minutes to deflate. It was almost comical, watching the mosquitoes trying to get blood out of that yellow balloon! Later, I tried different colors, from white to green, to orange, blue and red. It did not seem to make very much difference, so long as the stale breath was leaking, but when I tied a balloon outside which had not been punctured, only a few mosquitoes were attracted to it and these left in a short time.

After beaching the canoe, we climb the slope that leads to the campsite, for we want to get under cover in the well-ventilated tent. As we break out of a patch of pines, we see the lazy, circling shape of a turkey vulture. We pause to watch the big bird and he, in turn, appears to become interested in our movements, for he circles overhead and comes a little lower. We can clearly see his lean red head that moves continuously from side to side as he searches for carrion.

In the air, he is all beautiful motion, that black scavenger; on the ground, or seen close up, he is repulsive. He carries with him the odor of his food, the sweet-rank fetor of death that has become impregnated in his feathers. His beak is hideous, his gaping nostrils unusually large for a bird. The pasty-white patches under his eyes form wrinkled half-circles, like the puffy bags left by debauch upon some evil and aging lecher.

That is the turkey vulture on the ground. But look at the bird now, as he soars so effortlessly up there against the blue! Can any flying thing perform with such grace those intricate, fluid glides and spirals? The six-foot wings are held outstretched and still, but for the quivering of the wind through the slotted feathers at the tips, that the vulture can open and close to control his spirals. Now he seems to be hanging motionless upon an updraft, then he spirals again, performing his aerial ballet for our benefit. With a few flaps, slow and casual, he rises, circling high and higher into the empty sky, until he is but a black speck that finally becomes too small for our eyes to follow.

Perched, the turkey vulture is an ugly bird.

A mile to the north of where we stand is the vulture's nest, built in a small cave that is hardly more than a hollow in a cluster of large rocks. But the word "nest" is a poor description of a vulture's birthplace, for the female lays her two yellowish-white eggs, blotched irregularly with brown spots, right on the bare ground. She sits on them for some thirty-six days while the young develop within them.

The harpy-like chicks come into the world on a surface that is still clean, but that will soon be soiled with the rotten juices of the carrion that is regurgitated for them by the parent birds. During the first week or so of their lives, it is quite tolerable for a human to watch the nest from close quarters, but it takes a strong stomach to approach near the young after these have been feeding for any length of time. The odor of decayed meat has, by the second week of their life, permeated the entire cave. But these strange hatchlings thrive on the diet of putrid, half-digested meat that the adults thrust down their gaping throats.

About two months after hatching, the gangling youngsters begin to try out their wings, jogging away clumsily with labored flappings until at last they lift off. Then, as though by magic, the ugly chicks become transformed into lithe, graceful fliers, masters of the air that are bent on a constant scavenger hunt.

Even though turkey vultures can usually see their food on the ground below, as often as not they seem to sniff it out, perhaps to determine whether it is "ripe" enough to allow them to tear it apart with their small talons, relatively weak feet and clumsy beaks.

Tests have shown that these birds can actually sniff out carrion that has been concealed from sight, provided the food is smelly enough, and it is believed that the gases of decomposition, rising in the air, quickly attract them. In fact, in other tests, gases that simulate the stench of decaying meat have also attracted turkey vultures, though no actual food was in sight. Such tests may help to explain the uncanny ability of these birds to appear soon after the death of an animal.

On the wing, the turkey vulture is lighter than his relatives. During calm days, he sails effortlessly, using the warm updrafts to keep him suspended. In rougher weather, the vulture rocks rather unsteadily as he soars, but is well able to continue his beautiful spiraling.

When the vulture has gone, we proceed to the tent, to eat and to rest. About three o'clock we make ready for the late afternoon watch in the blind, wondering what new bird will be entered in our log before this day is over.

Chattering Flotilla

We hear them as we paddle towards the rock island, though we cannot see them. By their quackings, we know there are a number of ducks concealed within the reeds at the southern end of the lake, and, as we settle once more within the sack-cloth shelter, we hope that we shall be able to watch some of these waterfowl.

It is less hot now, and there is a fair breeze that helps to keep the mosquitoes away. For a time we sit and listen to the whispering of a young poplar that grows near our blind. The breeze rustles through its long-stemmed leaves and causes them to shake and to rub against one another, creating a pleasant little sound. The water, too, calls softly as the wind causes it to lap against the rocks and against the peeled sticks of the beaver lodge. Presently we see two dark shapes swimming towards us.

The muskrats are coming, one ahead of the other, some fifty feet apart, each undoubtedly aware of the other's presence, but showing no desire for companionship. One of them, the leading rat, alters course and begins to swim diagonally for the beaver dam; the other keeps on going, and soon we see its sleek head drift past our blind. When the rats are gone, a bullfrog pops up from under the water, rests his fat forelimbs on a lily leaf for a few moments and then swims away, kicking out with his long back legs, to disappear among the reeds.

For a time there is nothing facing us but water and reeds and the forest, then we hear a low quacking and we see three black duck drakes approaching. We dub them males because

of their greenish-yellow bills, for, though male and female of this species are almost identical in plumage, the bill of the female is usually darker, a dusky olive-green. Even the bill color is no sure guide, because there are variations, but this is summer and the drakes are free to roam in small bands, while the ducks are still busy with their broods; so we feel safe in recording these three as drakes.

These are dark brown birds, their somber plumage relieved only slightly by the lighter neck and the azure patches on their wings. They swim past us, darting this way and that, probing every likely bit of floating matter and sometimes being rewarded by some morsel of food. When they have gone by, we can still hear them for some time, gossiping in low tones amongst themselves. They are grounded just now, because they are in the molt and their new wing feathers have not yet fully developed.

Again there is empty water in front of our blind, but not for long. A female black duck comes into view, leading her flotilla of yellow-brown babies. Their loud peepings rise above even the sharp quacking of their mother. They paddle around our small island, searching for food in shallow places where even the tiny young can forage on the bottom by tipping their bodies, tail up.

Black ducks are sturdy birds, keen of perception and perhaps the wariest of all the surface-feeding ducks. They and their close relatives, the mallards, with whom they sometimes interbreed, arrive early in the spring and stay late, often until the frosts of autumn sheet their waterways with thin ice. Even then, a few linger until the ice has become so heavy that too much effort is needed to beat open a swimming hole with their wings. Then, at last, the stragglers follow the early starters to wintering grounds farther south, where there is open water.

In the spring, the courtship rituals of the drakes are long and elaborate, though the dance of the blacks is not as prolonged or quite as intricate as that of the mallards. After the all-male dancing, each bird showing off and seeming to com-

Black duck

pete with the others, each drake seeks out a female and literally chases her all over the place. Both birds appear to enjoy the wild dashes hither and yon that are accompanied by much splashing of wings and repeated calls.

Then comes the nesting. The female may build a down-lined nest within the shelter of the cat-tails, or she may choose a brushy clearing, concealed by low shrubs and some distance from water. She may even decide to nest in a tree, as the wood ducks do.

Wherever she builds her nest, the black duck will lay between six and twelve greenish-buff or creamy white eggs—the most usual number is nine—and she will incubate them for about twenty-eight days. Those ducklings born in a nest on the ground or on the water, simply scurry away and begin their life on lake or pond or river, but those that are born in a tree nest must face a rather fearful ordeal. The mother does not feed them up there and she can't carry them down, so the young must jump! Fortunately, they weigh so little, and the forest floor is usually so soft, that they come to no harm from their descent. Afterwards they waddle along behind their mother, as she leads them to the water.

The black duck and her young are feeding opposite our blind now. Suddenly, something startles the mother. It may be the slightly flapping canvas of our blind or perhaps even the sound of our breathing, for these birds appear to have very keen ears; whatever it is, she becomes alarmed. She calls to her eight young ones and the little ducks streak away towards the rushes, pumping their downy wings as they go, and giving the impression that they are actually running on the water, rather than frantically paddling with their small, webbed feet. The female hurries after them, and the group soon disappears into the shelter of the thick wall of green.

Soon after, we hear the mother black lead her babies out once more, but she keeps clear of the blind and we don't see them. But then a wood duck swims sedately into view, a drake who still preserves in his feathers some of the glories of his mating colors, a little shabby now, for he, like the blacks, is molting. We log his presence and, as we are doing so, he is joined by seven other drakes and the squadron spends some time swimming within our field of vision.

Although it is obvious that they are not very hungry, probably having fed well within the reeds and rushes where they sat out the worst of the day's heat, they are still interested in food and now one, then another, will break away from the group to go in pursuit of some aquatic animal.

One of the drakes comes close to our rock island, intent on a small frog that rests on a lily pad. The frog seems unaware of the duck's approach and continues to sit unwinking, immobile. But, as the duck is almost upon him, the little frog moves with speed, leaping into the safety of the water long before the drake is within striking distance. The duck sees the movement and hurries uselessly.

When he reaches the leaf upon which the frog had rested, he nibbles at it tentatively, running one edge between his mandibles, as though half expecting to find the frog. As he lifts the leaf out of the water, a backswimmer darts away. Quickly the wood duck lunges, misses once, spurs forward and grabs the beetle before it can get away. A small morsel, but it satisfies the drake, who may feel he has not entirely wasted his energies. He turns and rejoins the others.

The wood duck is, without a doubt, the most beautiful of all the waterfowl—at least, that is my firm view! At the height of the breeding season, the magnificent drakes glow with iridescent hues which are accented by stripes of pure white. The colors are really beyond description, enlivening the wilderness with blue and green and bronze, ruby and yellow and mauve. They are a sight capable of thrilling all of us.

Wood ducks, unlike mallards and black ducks, who pick their mates after their arrival in the spring, pair off at their winter feeding grounds. It is the female who then leads the male back to the place of her choosing, perhaps the area in which she was born, or where she nested last year.

In any event, within the forest the female wood duck searches for a suitable nesting tree—one that offers a cavity such as a hollow trunk or limb, or a large, unused woodpecker hole. The site she chooses may be as high as fifty feet from

the ground, or only three or four feet up. Within the hole she lays her eggs and some twenty-eight days later the downy chicks hatch; then, incredibly, they scale the inside wall of their nest with the aid of very sharp claws, and flop lightly to the ground. The nesting tree may be near water, but it may just as easily be deep in the forest; then, as the mother escorts her brood to lake or river they stop often to feed, picking up whatever the forest floor offers.

Wood ducks often leave the water to go foraging in the woods and at quiet times it is possible to hear the chatter of a feeding family, the slender voices of the downies mixing with the chattering squeals of the adult birds, which, when alarmed, emit a loud and piercing cry: *whoo—oo-eek!*

Our first day in the blind is spent. Dusk has come to the lake, though it is not yet dark. The birds of day call more softly as they settle in the trees and bushes; the ducks quack hoarsely. The whip-poor-wills call their name over and over, the loons laugh wildly and the nighthawks fill the sky with their strange, nasal cries.

We leave the blind and are grateful for the exercise after being cooped up for so long, sitting most of the time on small stools and needing to remain quiet for fear of startling the birds. We are sweat-streaked, weary, hungry and not a little itchy, but we shall return tomorrow to continue our observations. Now, as we board the canoe and push away from the rock island, we think of a refreshing evening swim and of a good supper, followed by hot coffee sipped contemplatively by the campfire as we listen to the night. Then sleep, sound and dreamless.

Wood duck

Perky Gymnast

By sunrise, we are again concealed inside the blind; we have
already made our first entry in the log. As the sun tipped the
eastern trees and gained strength, we watched for a time
without seeing any life at all, except, of course, for the
ubiquitous mosquitoes. Then we saw a muskrat on the shore,
waddling quickly for the water, and we watched him slip into
it and swim a little way. Then he dived and we noted the
bubbles that lingered a few moments over the place where he
went under.

Near our rock, on a fluffed-out cat-tail, a white-faced hornet has alighted with a captive fly. The black and white
predator sits on its downy platform and holds the fly with its
forelegs, its jaws busy. The fly's wings have already been
removed, nipped off neatly by the hornet's powerful pincers,
and now the big insect detaches the legs, one by one. The
hornet then begins to eat the fly, twirling it as though it were
a tiny cob of corn, and in a few moments only the head remains. This the hornet discards, and then it preens itself fas-
tidiously, wiping its face and antennae and wings with its thin
legs. In another moment it has gone, disturbing a few shreds
of cat-tail down that float slowly towards the water.

As we watch, the cat-tails are disturbed, set to moving
slightly, but at first we cannot see through the forest of stems.
Then we spot a tiny bird, streaked brown and black on top,
light underneath; there is a pronounced white stripe over the
eye. It clings with both feet to a cat-tail stem as it searches for
insects. "Long-billed marsh wren," we note in our log.

The four-inch bird carries its short tail erect and its longish

Long-billed marsh wren

legs seem to emerge from the very end of its chunky body, as though they have been set too far back, almost at the very root of its tail. It is unafraid, aware of our blind and perhaps of our presence, but too busy with its own affairs to bother about the strange structure that sits on the rock. With jerky movements it slides up and down the cat-tail stems and picks off insects that are too small for us to see. Then it disappears within the cover of stems, only to hop out again, perch on a leaning stalk and fix the blind with one beady black eye. As though in greeting, it sings, a reedy, gurgling little song that ends in a long, guttural rattle. Afterwards, it disappears again and we hear the rustle of its passage as it retreats within the cat-tails.

The long-billed marsh wren sings its strange song day or night, from its shelter within brackish coastal marshes or in cat-tail patches far inland. The male of this species, like all wrens, is given to the building of dummy nests, while the female fashions a structure shaped rather like a coconut,

219

which she anchors to several reeds or cat-tail stems. She constructs her home with long strips of vegetation and lines it with cat-tail down, feathers, grasses, and any other soft material she can find. This largish ball of vegetation has an entrance at the side, and within its shelter the female lays five or six brown eggs that are spotted with darker brown. The young are hatched in thirteen days.

Marsh wrens, of which there are two species, the long-billed and the short-billed, feed on a variety of insects and consume large quantities of mosquito and black fly larvae, which they peck right out of the water. They are assiduous little hunters that seem to be forever on the go and, although they usually remain within the concealment of the plants, where they find most of their food, they are not particularly shy.

The short-billed marsh wren is lighter-colored than the long-billed, has a streaky appearance on the head and back, and lacks the white eye-stripe of its near relative. It haunts wet meadows and grassy marshes, building a ball-shaped nest that is smaller and rounder than the long-bill's.

Now the little wren has disappeared and, replacing the quiet rustle of its movements in the cat-tails, we hear the strident voice of a pileated woodpecker. It calls once only, and a few moments later a powerful barrage of blows tells us that the big cock-of-the-north has found a tree containing hidden insects.

Blending with the big woodpecker's drumming, we hear the screams of a flicker, its raucous, strident voice approaching. Presently we see it, and we note it in the log. "Common flicker," we write, noting that it is a male, recognized as such by the black "mustache" that slants across its cheeks. The flicker swoops and dips in characteristic woodpecker flight, showing its white rump, and passes over our blind and out of sight.

As the bird flew over, we clearly saw the golden-yellow undersides of its wings and tail, which gave it its former, more descriptive name of "yellow-shafted flicker". In the West,

Common flicker

---

where its wing-linings are salmon-red, it used to be considered a separate species and was called the red-shafted flicker. Many variations in wing color take place when eastern and western individuals interbreed, and on the western edge of the Great Plains flickers with orange-yellow underwings are often seen. The western bird also differs from the eastern in having no red on the back of the head, and the male has a red mustache instead of a black one.

Whatever the color of their wing linings, these woodpeckers are voracious insect eaters and wage almost ceaseless war on many harmful species. They have a particular fondness for ants, eating, when the hunting is good, several thousand in a day.

Marsh Pumper

As we are pondering these things, our train of thought is broken by a strange, deep, sucking sound issuing from the cat-tail patch. Two pairs of field glasses are pointed in that direction and we carefully scan the thick growth for any strange shape or movement. No luck.

Just as we are about to give up, the sound comes again. It is as if someone were driving a heavy stake into the mud. It comes from the right-hand side of the patch, as we are facing it. We zero in on the smaller area, and wait.

After a few minutes, there is a movement in the forest of stems, and out steps a large, striped, brown bird with a long bill and fairly long, greenish legs. "American bittern," we note.

The heron-like bird strides slowly a little way along the edge of the cat-tails, and stops. It points its bill at the shallow water and remains motionless for some time. Suddenly, with a quick thrust of the beak, it snaps up a frog and swallows it.

We watch it hunting in this way for some half an hour, then, with great dignity, the bird moves into the cat-tails and is gone from our sight.

The call of the American bittern is described by a variety of three-syllabled expressions. One listener says the bird's voice sounds like *oong-ka-choonk,* another describes it as *pump-er-lunk,* and so on. In fact, it is doubtful that any written com-

American bittern in camouflage posture

The bittern's pumping calls are repeated again and again during the breeding season at any time of day and often at night, though the bird utters his deep sounds, more sparingly, throughout the spring and early summer. The slough pump, or thunder pump, as the bittern is variously called, has another note, a croak not unlike that of the blue heron, but more rapid and repeated three or four times, usually when the bird has been alarmed.

Bitterns nest deep in the marshlands on nearly-floating platforms of dead cat-tail stems, where the female lays between four and six buff-colored eggs. She sits on the eggs for about twenty-four days and afterwards feeds her young on regurgitated frogs, snakes, fish, crayfish and other small water animals.

These largish birds, about thirty inches in length, breed across most of the continent, ranging as far north as Great Slave Lake, in the Northwest Territories, and as far south as the Mexican border. In winter they are not found north of Illinois and Virginia.

We are now getting restless in the confinement of our sacking enclosure; the weather is hot and humid and the woods are cooler and offer many attractions. Shall we stay on here, or shall we go walking? The temptation is too strong. We shall go, to follow the game trails quietly and to listen and watch for other birds, perhaps to photograph some if we are lucky. What about the mosquitoes, you say? Well, we must endure them, and the deer flies and the big horse flies; they are part of this wilderness, as much a part as the birds and all the other life that we shall encounter as we walk.

Well sprayed with insect repellent, wearing floppy hats to protect us from the sun, and jeans and long-sleeved shirts to ward off bites and bramble-scratches, we shall set off in the morning, early, so we can cover a reasonable distance before the sun broils down and drives us back to the shelter of the tent.

The Rose-Breast

Today we are looking for the songbirds: the warblers, the thrushes, the sparrows, and many others. No longer do we have to sit cramped and sweating under the sackcloth; instead we roam through the woods and clearings, walking softly, always alert for some new bird.

The sun is past the tree-tops and we have already crossed the lake by walking along the lip of the beaver dam; now we are stopped behind a brushy alder and we watch a sturdy bird with a bright rose V-patch on its breast. It is a little smaller than a robin and has a heavy, whitish beak. We are please to have "collected" a rose-breasted grosbeak for our log. The rose patch tells us at once that this is an adult male, so do the charcoal head and back, splashed with white on the wings and tail. He has white underparts, and bluish legs and feet. His mate, who is probably somewhere in the vicinity— for by this date the young must already be born—is a dull, olive-brown color streaked with white, and has a conspicuous white band over each eye.

The grosbeak is perched on a poplar branch, singing his melodious song which is not unlike that of a robin, but somewhat warmer and richer. He is one of the few male birds sporting conspicuous feathers that helps his mate to incubate the eggs. He evidently enjoys singing, for he does it continually, sometimes even while he is sitting on the eggs.

Grosbeaks of this species nest in trees or tall shrubbery, placing the rather flat, loosely-made structure between five and fifteen feet from the ground. The four or five young arrive flesh-pink and scrawny, but after a few days they are well

bination of letters can ever effectively describe the sound made by this large, but self-effacing bird; but its voice is absolutely unmistakable and unlike any other bird sound.

The bittern, in effect, belches its call. Going through some rather violent body contortions, this marsh dweller swallows air in great gulps, distending its crop and throat like an oddly-shaped balloon, then it releases the trapped air in a series of loud, deep-toned burps that can be heard for a mile or more on a quiet day.

More often than not, the bittern is heard but not seen. The bird is shy and, because of its well-camouflaged body, which blends completely into its marshy haunts, and its habit of freezing into immobility, when it senses danger, head and neck stiffly erect and beak pointing at the sky, even a careful observer will often fail to see it. But even in this strange posture it is always watching. Its eyes seem to be fixed on ball bearings and can be focused backwards or forwards, up or down, so that while the bittern is frozen with its head pointing up, its eyes swivel around in their sockets and keep an intruder constantly in view. Go too close to the bird and it flaps up awkwardly, to fly away to another feeding place.

A word of warning to people who might come across an injured bittern: this bird has a long, strong and very sharp beak, which it uses mainly for gathering its food, but which it will also use in self-defense. Anybody who stoops over a cornered bittern and attempts to pick it up is quite likely to get stabbed in the face by the dangerous beak and serious injury can result, particularly to the eyes. The bird can be handled, but it should always be done with caution and the fierce beak should be firmly secured before any attempt is made to pick up an injured bird.

Some authorities claim that the bittern deliberately seeks out the human face in such circumstances, but this seems unlikely. It is more reasonable to suppose that the face, because it is the part that presents itself most closely when a curious observer bends over the bird, is therefore a convenient target for the bird's defensive attacks. In any event, if left alone, the bittern is completely harmless and wants nothing more than to stay out of human paths.

Rose-breasted grosbeak, male

covered with fluffy white down, for all the world like living powder puffs.

After the chicks are raised, during early autumn, the male assumes the more somber hues of his mate on the head, neck and back, though he keeps his sooty black on tail and wings. Then it is hard to distinguish him from an immature bird. In any plumage, he shows at least some trace of his pink chest patch, and the linings of his wings have a rosy hue.

These birds eat as much animal protein as they do vegetable matter, pursuing and capturing insects as readily as they dine on wild fruit (or cultivated fruit, come to that!), seeds and nuts. But if they raid an occasional garden, they more than pay for the fruit that they eat by their fondness for locusts, potato beetles and cankerworms, to name but a few of the insect pests that disappear within a grosbeak's crop.

The rose-breast belongs to the Fringillidae, a large family

The female grosbeak looks very different from her mate.

of mainly seed-eating birds that includes grosbeaks, finches, sparrows and buntings. Many of the birds in this family are brightly colored, except the sparrows, which are usually quietly clad in shades of brown.

One of the best known of the grosbeaks is the cardinal, that brilliant red, crested bird with black around his bill. His lady, though more subdued in her brownish tones, still sports a red crest and has some of her mate's color on her tail. In both sexes the large, heavy bill is red.

Another favorite is the evening grosbeak with its lemon-yellow color, complemented by a brownish head and black and white wings. This is a widespread bird, breeding across Canada from northern British Columbia to New Brunswick, in latitudes north of the larger Great Lakes, and southward in the mountains to California and South Carolina. In winter, it wanders in flocks through southern Canada and most of the United States.

The evening grosbeak does not only appear at sundown, as

its name might suggest; it feeds during all the daylight hours. It has a special fondness for the seeds of Manitoba maple and choke cherry, and will often come to the bird feeder for sunflower seeds.

We think of these other birds as we watch and listen to the rose-breast, who is still perched on his branch and still sings his cheerful song. As we watch, he is joined by his mate and the two sit side by side. She is silent, but he continues with his song for a time; when he stops, he leans towards her and gently nibbles her head feathers. Then the two suddenly take off, leaving the branch in unison and disappearing into the shelter of a thick grove of balsam trees.

The Mewer

We walk again, threading our way through country that is sparsely treed but heavy in undergrowth. Here, there is a profusion of blueberry bushes. Their fruit is plump-purple and sweet and we pause to eat, stripping the round fruit from the branchlets with ease, for this has been a good blueberry year.

As we munch, the purple juice staining our lips and fingers, we hear a plaintive mewing coming from a small valley to our right. This depression is full of tangled growth, a mixture of poplar and birch and alder and willow, all young trees, that thin out as the land slopes towards a small marshy area. Growing in the marsh, the alders predominate and it is from this thicket that the mewing originates. It sounds like a lost kitten, but out here? No, we know better. This is the voice of the catbird.

This dark gray bird is between eight and nine inches long and is of sleek proportions, with a longish tail. In a good light we may see a black stripe along the crown of its head and a rusty patch under its tail. We stop and we squat, keeping still, searching the tangle of green with our glasses. We notice that the mewing is now and then interrupted by a musical medley of scrambled notes.

At last we are rewarded for our search. There, perched on a stub in a dead alder, is our catbird. Its feet grip the smooth

Catbird

branch tightly, its body is held in a crouch, and the rather broad tail points upward. Its wings are drooping at its sides, a characteristic pose of this gifted songster.

As well as singing his own wide range of notes and phrases, the catbird takes pleasure in imitating the songs of other forest birds. So enthusiastic a musician is he, that he is even likely to sing in the dead of night. When walking through the woods after the sun has set, one may hear soft twitterings that are familiar, yet somehow strange. As one is puzzling as to their origin, the catbird may call again, in another voice; and so on. Sometimes it is not until he lets slip a mewing note, that we recognize the identity of the singer.

Now, because he is disturbed by our presence, he is mewing, his tail is raised and he holds the quick-get-away crouch, for he is a rather shy and timid bird. When he is unaware of observers, he usually holds his tail pointing downwards, almost tucked under his body, while he sings. But sometimes the catbird becomes quite bold, for no apparent reason, and then he perches on top of a bush or tree and sings his repertoire in full view. He always sounds a bit mad to me—something of an unpredictable clown.

Winging northward at night from his wintering grounds, which may be as far south as Central America, the catbird male goes directly to the area where he intends to breed. His first job, once he has regained the vigor he has lost during his long flight, is to stake out his home territory and tell his rivals in the forest that he will fight to hold his land. He does this by emitting a series of mews, mixed with warblings and impromptu notes, but he makes his challenge clear and he is absolutely prepared to back it up with beak and wings and feet. When the females arrive, he wastes no time in wooing the mate of his choice.

The courtship is fast and furious. Sighting an attractive female, he begins a mad dashing through the underbrush; it looks aimless, but has a definite purpose—the hot pursuit of the coy female, who is just as nimble as he and leads him a merry chase. Once he is sure that he has captured her attention, he alights on a branch and struts purposefully up and down, wings drooping at his sides, tail up. Every so often he stops and bursts into song. If the female heeds his antics, the pair settle down to domesticity.

Now the male tells the world that he has won a mate. He sings repeatedly day and night, while his spouse is busy nest-building. First of all she chooses a site that is low to the ground and located within dense cover. Once she has found a place that is to her liking, she begins building her nest, gathering dead sticks, pieces of bark, leaves and grass, weaving and tamping industriously, while Mr. Catbird continues to tell the world that he has found his love for the year. When the female has fashioned the main structure of her nest, she begins to line it neatly, using plant rootlets, the soft, inner shreds of dead tree bark, feathers and bits of moss. Then she lays three to five green-blue eggs and incubates them for about thirteen days. The babies come into the world red and naked and wobbly, big-headed and blind, with soft beaks that seem to be forever opening to receive food.

At this stage, both birds are kept busy hunting insects, upon which their young subsist almost entirely, and if the father now and then breaks away to feast on wild fruits, well, who can blame him? Even though he sometimes plays truant, he is quick to respond to his mate's cry of distress should she be threatened. In fact, catbirds possess a social instinct shared by few birds and they will often rush to the rescue of babies that are not their own, quite readily adopting a brood that has been orphaned by some predator.

Despite the territorial rivalry that exists between males, these birds will band together to repel a predator, be it snake or hawk or crow, responding to the alarm call and hurrying to the scene. I once saw no fewer than nine catbirds attacking a crow that had flown over the nesting area of a pair of them. The battle was preceded by the furious mews and the quick upward flight of the two birds who felt threatened. Within moments, seven more catbirds had flown in from various directions and the hapless crow was harried, rather like some cumbersome bomber being attacked by fighters. The catbirds did not cease their diving and pecking until the crow was well clear of their area, and by that time he had lost a number of his feathers.

When the young catbirds have been raised and are able to take care of themselves, the mated pair usually break up and the male changes his song. Now he indulges in a clear, soft trilling, a "whisper song" quite unlike his lively summer sounds.

The male that we are watching stops mewing, stoops a little more and jumps off his perch, diving deep into the tangles of his thicket. As we move away, his plaintive mewing follows us for a time.

Stealthy Songster

The area through which we are now walking is ideal bird habitat and it resounds continuously to the bustle of their activities. The ground is covered with blueberries and strawberries, one taking over where the other leaves off; choke cherry trees are plentiful and the clusters of tart fruits are already turning dark-red ripe; beaver ponds and marshes dot the landscape, while a mixture of evergreen and deciduous forest extends to all points of the compass. Here, there is an abundance of vegetable and insect life for the birds, plenty of nesting materials, cover in which to hide and lots of water. Little wonder, then, that so many species fly this way each spring and remain until the autumn colors put the first blush on the broadleaves.

We are walking at this moment on a ridge of granite that has not yet been conquered by the creeping moss. The rock is colored a subdued pink and in places inlays of quartz and feldspar run through it in lines that are too straight to have occurred by accident; they seem to have been laid out by some giant with set square and ruler. In truth, nature did this during some prehistoric upheaval of the earth. Great cracks appeared in the granite, and molten rock poured upwards, settled and cooled, leaving these distinct markings, known to the geologist as intrusions.

On our right, there is a small valley filled with trees and shrubs and carpeted by moss and ferns and a variety of colorful mushrooms; on our left, there is a large beaver pond on which we can see the ragged outlines of three beaver lodges and no less than nine muskrat houses. The beaver dam is

ahead of us and we can hear the music of the water as it slips over the top. Alder and sweet gale line the pond edges, and water-lilies fill the surface, so that the whole looks like a huge vase filled with yellow and white blooms.

On a dead stub, at the very top, a red-winged blackbird is singing, silhouetted against the sun. Somewhere on the other side of the pond a bittern pumps its booming cry, while warblers of many kinds fill the woods with their music. We walk quietly, entranced with the life around us, intending to cross the beaver dam and to roam on the far side of the pond, where there is a huge cat-tail marsh that is also full of bird life. But we are arrested before we get to the lip of the dam, by a sharp *chip* that comes from a group of young poplars. The single, sharp call is followed by a happy, tuneful song.

Some of the verbal interpretations of bird songs are far-fetched and difficult to translate by those who have never heard the actual sounds, but the brown thrasher's call is an easy one to interpret. Clearly the bird says: *Drop it, drop it! Cover-it-up, cover-it-up! Pull-it-up, pull-it-up!* Each phrase is repeated once, unlike the jumbled syllables of the catbird.

Here is a bird that is shy and careful in its actions, yet brilliant in its singing. Like its musical relatives, the catbird and the mockingbird, it often takes parts of other birds' songs and weaves them into an impromptu sonata. I have always felt a special affection for the brown thrasher, who goes about his affairs so tunefully, yet moves so easily that unless he is singing his presence is often undetected.

My first acquaintance with this bird was in Florida, in an area of everglades south of the Tamiami Trail. I had been sitting on a levée, watching a number of wood ibis (or, more correctly, wood storks), as they gyrated unsteadily in a tree, clacking their great bills and flapping their beautiful, black-edged wings. The big, snowy-white birds had come flying in from somewhere and landed, one at a time, in the tree. They were too far away for an effective photograph, but close

Brown thrasher

Young birds must be fed every fifteen minutes from dawn to dark.

enough for careful observation through my field glasses. I was fascinated by them and regretted that this was my last day in the 'glades; it would have been interesting to spend some more time studying these impressive creatures.

Engrossed in watching the ibises, I failed at first to hear the raspy *chip* that came from a bush near which I was squatting. Then, as the single syllable was repeated, it intruded on my consciousness. I turned slowly and found myself being closely examined by a bird with a bright brown back, a brown-streaked white breast and large yellow eyes. His tail was long, his beak slightly curved. He was a little larger than a robin. He seemed as interested in me as I had been in the ibis and, as though in greeting, he launched his tuneful song.

I chuckled with pleasure and spoke softly to him, though fully expecting him to fly away. But he stayed, eyed me more intently and sang again. When he had finished telling me to *pull-it-up!,* etcetera, he treated me to a wide repertoire of other phrases, then he chipped once more, bobbed his long tail and flew away.

238

Now we are hearing another of his kind, and we stop and search for the singer, sweeping the poplars slowly with our field glasses until at last we see him. But for the difference in geography and habitat, he could be the same bird who greeted me that day in Florida. He sits in the same pose, whistling the same melody, and moving his tail up and down in the same way.

The brown thrasher becomes subdued in the spring when he is joined by a female, singing more quietly, as though the imminent cares of parenthood are giving him pause for thought. After the young have hatched, in the bulky nest which is perhaps on the ground but more likely in a thorny thicket, the parents carry an endless variety of insects to pop into the ever-open mouths. Thrashers seem to have a special fondness for juicy caterpillars and I have watched them devour dozens at a single sitting.

The one we are watching sings again for us, utters his short *chip* and hops to a new branch, where he begins to scan the ground with interest. He flies down and we lose sight of him for a moment, but soon he comes flying into view, a large grasshopper secure in his beak. Away he goes with his prize, probably back to the nest and the young birds that must be almost fully fledged by this time of year.

Beauty on the Wing

We cross the beaver dam, walking securely on the mounded mud and sticks that the beaver have wedged so firmly to a width of three feet at the top. As we brush past the alders and willows that line the other side of the stream, we tread carefully to avoid crushing the profusion of wildflowers that grow underfoot. For a moment a marsh wren appears, bobs once and flies away. In the sky, a red-shouldered hawk is gliding; the light-colored "windows" on the undersides of his wings are clearly visible—a good identification mark. We put him down in our log and move on.

Now we are on craggy ground. Boulders of all sizes and shapes litter the landscape, and between them the ground is covered with blueberry bushes. Ahead of us, on an outcrop of rock, a giant white pine has somehow managed to find enough soil for its needs. We walk towards it.

Moments later, we have stopped again, arrested by a great noise coming from a patch of blueberries. The dry rustlings and scrapings sound too noisy for a bird, but in a moment a male towhee pops out from among the berry bushes.

This songster is quite capable of making a big racket, despite being smaller than a robin. Scratching with sturdy feet, like a small chicken, tossing leaves aside with his short but useful beak, the towhee makes enough noise for five or six other birds, as he searches for insects or vegetable matter on the forest floor.

Now he feeds on blueberries while we watch him and, though he is aware of our presence, he shows no signs of nervousness. He sings—*to-whee, to-whee*—a bright and cheerful

Rufous-sided towhee

chirping, the sound of which has given him his name.

His heavy beak is black, his eyes, ruby-red; on the chest and back and wings he is mostly black, with flashes of white. His rufous-brown sides contrast with the black of his back and the white of his belly.

He sings once more and looks at us, then turns his attention back to the berries. He pecks away, eating rapidly as he teeters up and down the fruit-loaded branches. At this moment, his mate appears. Where the male is black, she is a light cinnamon. She has the same white on her belly and the same ruby eyes and rather heavy beak.

Each bird is busy cramming food into its crop, for itself and for the six young birds that wait in the loosely-built nest, which is lined with fine grasses and tufts of animal hair. I found the nest a couple of weeks ago, on another morning ramble, being attracted to it by the comings and goings of the female. At the time, it had contained six white eggs that were dotted with brown.

Cedar waxwing

We walk on now, leaving the towhees to their feast, and as we approach a large choke cherry, we see a handsome bird feeding greedily on the fruit. "Cedar waxwing," we scribble hastily, and we stop to admire this crested, black-masked and very beautiful bird. The waxwing's feathers are so sleek, they seem almost to have been painted on its body. He (or she, for the sexes are clad alike) is brown on his head and back, shading almost to black on his rump, the ends of his wings, and his tail. Bordering the end of his tail is a band of buttercup yellow. His underparts are greenish-yellow. Through the field glasses, in the clear morning light, we can see a red line on each wing. These are made by little blobs of hard material, something like sealing-wax, that for some reason yet unknown decorates the tips of some of the wing-feathers.

At this time of year, when the nestlings are not quite able to take care of themselves, one will often see individual waxwings foraging for fruit or insects on which to feed their young. But when the cares of parenthood do not intrude, it is not unusual for a flock of a dozen or more to feed or rest in the same tree.

Waxwings appear to enjoy each other's company and they indulge in a charming, if mysterious, ritual. Sitting several on a branch, all facing in the same direction, one of the birds passes a berry, or perhaps a large insect, to his neighbor, who nibbles it and passes it to the next in line, and so on until the food is eventually consumed, a bit being taken by each bird in turn. There appears to be no serious purpose in this rite; perhaps it is just a pleasant social custom.

The cedar waxwing has a wide distribution in North America. It occurs, during the breeding season, from south-eastern Alaska to Newfoundland and southward to California, Utah, Oklahoma, Illinois, Alabama and Georgia. In winter, its range is from the northern United States and a few localities in southern Canada, to Panama.

Cedar waxwings mate late in the year, usually waiting for the berries to ripen, for, though they eat a large number of insects, they seem to prefer feeding their young on a diet that consists mainly of fruit. After the mating, a nest is built in a tree or a tall shrub, at heights varying from five to forty or fifty feet. The young hatch in about twelve days, from spotted, grayish or greenish-blue eggs.

All waxwings are wanderers, except when they are nesting, but the habit is most pronounced in the cedar waxwing's somewhat larger cousin, the bohemian waxwing. This is an even more beautiful bird, resembling its commoner relative, but having also an orange tinge around its beak and some white and yellow markings on its wings. Under the tail, where the cedar waxwing is white, the bohemian is cinnamon-red.

Bohemian waxwings nest throughout British Columbia, Alaska and the Yukon and in the western part of the North-west Territories, south to northern Manitoba and Saskatchewan, Alberta, Washington, Idaho and Montana. In winter, it ranges from southern British Columbia right across southern Canada and the northern United States; at this time of year, one never knows just where a flock of bohemian waxwings may turn up.

Invisible Sprite

One autumn, as I was walking through the woods, I found a dead woodcock and, because I had never seen one of these birds up close, I examined it with care. This one had evidently been shot, during the hunting season which had just ended, and had been left, wounded, to die a lingering death. It was thin and several pellet wounds in its legs and thighs had festered. As usual when I come across examples of wanton destruction by my own kind, I felt a sharp anger rise within me. Too many birds are wounded each year and left to die, just as far too many become victims of lights and tall buildings during their migrations.

As I studied the dead woodcock, I was struck by the position of its large eyes, which are placed high up, almost on the top of its head. I was surprised at first, but when I remembered the bird's manner of feeding, I once again marveled at the way in which nature has adapted each species for survival in its own special habitat.

Woodcock, which are relatives of the sandpipers, are mottled, red-brown birds that frequent brushy wetlands. There they feed almost entirely on earthworms, which they locate and grasp in the soft soil with a most effective tool—a very long beak with a flexible tip. As a result, the woodcock spends a great deal of its time with its head down, probing for its food. In this stance, were its eyes in the orthodox position, the bird would be almost blind and would quickly fall prey to hawk or fox or other predator. So nature created an adaptation and gave the woodcock eyes that are set high up and far back in its head; with these it can keep watch almost

American woodcock

full circle, while its beak is nearly buried in the forest soil. In fact, most of the members of the family Scolopacidae share this pecularity, for similar reasons, particularly the common snipe, which closely resembles the plumper, browner woodcock.

During the breeding season, the male woodcock performs an aerial ballet that is as graceful as it is fantastic. Usually at dusk, in an opening in the thicket, the male woodcock begins his performance. First, he utters a loud *peent!*, rather like the cry of a nighthawk, as he struts pompously through the grass. He may repeat this note several times. Then his short, rounded wings beat quickly and make a whistling sound as he spirals upwards, as high as 200 feet, to hover and sing. The fluidity of the song is hard to capture in the written syllables: *chickaree, chickaree, chickaree, chickaree.* Reaching the climax of his solo, he zigzags rapidly downwards, emitting a series of chirping notes that have an almost metallic quality.

Back on firm ground again, he does a little more strutting

and calling, then up he goes once more. Meanwhile, one or more females are squatting or walking below, presumably admiring the cock bird's performance. Actually he is something of a roué, for he hopes to mate with as many of them as he can.

On nights of full moon, the woodcock may perform for hours without tiring, even all night, to the delight of those who know him; those who don't may wonder, on hearing these sounds during an evening stroll, what manner of sprite is making them.

Woodcock arrive early in the spring, often when the snow is still on the ground. The nest is a scanty affair of leaves carelessly raked together, in which the female lays her brownish eggs. She incubates them and raises the young without help from the male, who wanders away to continue feeding on earthworms wherever he can find them, often consuming half his own weight of worms in a night.

Because their favorite food is more active at night, woodcock spend more time feeding during darkness than in the daylight. After sun-up, they sit quietly on the ground, well camouflaged in their woods-colored feathers. If disturbed, they explode in fast flight, making a difficult target for a predator, whether animal or human.

Nevertheless, woodcock were almost brought to extinction by greedy hunters, who, before sensible regulations for their protection were introduced, gunned them down mercilessly. It was not unusual for a hunter to kill more than 100 of these remarkable birds in one day, using dogs and walking in lines through the birds' habitat. Today, fortunately, bag limits have been set and the birds are no longer in danger of being wiped out. Still, I would rather hear their song than the explosions of shotgun shells!

Looking at that dead woodcock, I thought of these things. I realized, too, that soon the last of the migrants would be gone—the sparrows, the finches, the hawks, other, more fortunate woodcock, all winging their way to warmer climes. And then I thought of the dangers they must face on their long journeys, including the presence of brightly-lit, man-made structures.

One night in fall, a number of years ago, I discovered at first hand how seriously artificial light can hinder the navigation of those birds that travel at night. I was living on a farm north of the city of Toronto and had installed a powerful light in the yard, the kind that switches itself on automatically at dusk and off again at the coming of daylight.

I had been sitting in the living room, reading, for some time and felt the need to stretch my legs. To my amazement, when I stepped out of the door I saw several hundreds of birds, some fluttering around the light, rather like big moths, and others walking about on the inch or so of early snow and scratching for food. Because of the confusion of so many birds, I was not able to make an accurate count of the different species, but there were woodcock, several kinds of sparrow, juncos, goldfinches, purple finches, snipe and several species of warblers. Seven assorted birds actually flew into the house, attracted, I suppose, by the light that came through the open door. Three of these were tree sparrows, one was a purple finch, one was a junco and two were goldfinches.

After I got them outside, I continued to be amazed, because none of the birds around the light and in the yard seemed to be aware of my presence. They flew around me, bumping into me, some landing on me, and yet they showed no fear. I was actually able to pick up a woodcock and it did not struggle while I held it, and none of the seven birds that had come into the house had fussed when I caught them and put them outside again.

I returned to the house and got a sack of mixed bird seed and returned to the light with it. As I started to scatter it in small piles on the snow, the birds began to feed, paying not the slightest attention to me. Several tree sparrows actually perched on the bag and picked up seeds as I was scattering the food.

I watched these birds for several hours and they alternately flew around the light and landed to feed. The night was heavily overcast, a snow sky, though it did not actually snow again until two days later. This, to my knowledge, was the first time that such a thing had happened during the two years since I had had the light installed, though it could have occurred while I was absent or asleep.

At three o'clock in the morning I stopped watching the birds. I went out and replenished the food supply, with the same results as before, then I went to bed. When I awoke at seven o'clock, I immediately looked out of the bedroom window. All the birds had gone. When I went outside, every last seed that I had put out was gone also. By actual measure, those birds had consumed 100 pounds of seed, for I had opened a new bag and had put out the entire contents.

I believe that a number of birds came to the light after I first noticed the melée, as though they, too, had been drawn down as they were flying overhead. But I cannot be certain of this because of the enormous confusion of flying shapes.

After this strange incident, I fully realized the great toll that our modern cities exact on migrating birds. Records show that as many as 50,000 birds have died in one night as a result of flying into lighted structures, such as television towers, aircraft beacons and skyscrapers. To date, little has been done to avert these disasters. Perhaps it is time for men to begin serious research into the ways and means of eliminating these terrible hazards to bird populations.

Magnificent Whooper

White smoke belched at the sky, rising in a straight, threatening plume and then spreading, rather like an atomic mushroom, as it was pushed by the ground heat. Particles of ash fell like snow. At the foot of that column of smoke, the wilderness was dying. It glowed red, illuminated by the fierce light of its own funeral pyre. The raging flames engulfed evergreen and broadleaf with equal abandon, raced up the trunks, blossomed their crowns and passed on, leaving a trail of black and smoldering stumps. And as the flames sped onwards, they sent forth sparks and embers that sought other trees and shrubs and grasses upon which to feed. This was the inferno that, in 1954, charged through Wood Buffalo National Park, that great tract of wilderness that begins in northern Alberta and spills into the Northwest Territories, to end just south of Great Slave Lake.

In the path of the fire stood a big birch tree. Its white bark hung in spirals, like old wallpaper peeling from the walls of a deserted house. A tiny fragment of fire drifted through the hot air, hung over the tree for a moment and then slid down, settling on a curl of bark. The spark, an advance guard of the fire, met ideal conditions. Already the forest in this area was seared by the heat, almost to the point of combustion. In an instant, a puff of black, greasy smoke sprang from the white bark. A thin, yellow flame took hold and suddenly became a streamer of fire that licked at the tree, picking up other loose curls of bark as it went upwards towards the green crown. The whole trunk exploded in flames, like a giant Roman can-

dle, projecting its own shower of live embers high into the air.

Each spark found something upon which to settle and feed and the fire raced on. Even the ground burned. The topsoil was composed of mulch, muskeg, deposited there by the ages and it was dry from weeks of sun. It would continue to burn for weeks to come. Even after the snow came it would still burn and spread, underground. Only the wet of returning spring would fully extinguish it.

As the flames advanced, birds and animals fled before them, crazed by the force they dread above all others and frantic in their haste to find sanctuary. Deer fled, wild-eyed with terror. A mother bear tried to lead her cubs out of danger, to a little lake, but the two babies could not keep up with her. She waited for them, but the sparks set fire to their fur and all three died in the inferno.

A bewildered snowy owl blundered into the path of the fire, clacking its beak in fear at the suffocating smoke and heat. It passed close to a burning spruce; the fire touched its soft feathers and curled them into molten, glossy blobs and the owl fell.

Like the owl, thousands of birds were burned to death that year, some smothered by the smoke and fumes, others incinerated as they flew. Yet, ironically, it was because of that fire that the nesting grounds of the whooping crane were discovered.

A government forester, returning in a helicopter after inspecting fire damage, spotted three whoopers in a marshy area—two adults and one fledgling, which had evidently survived the fire because of their watery habitat. A wave of excitement gripped conservationists all over the world. Since 1922, no evidence of nesting had been found. The birds had once nested on the prairies, but when the settlers arrived and marshes were drained and the lands were put to the plow, the big, spectacular cranes dwindled and finally all but disappeared.

In the spring of 1955 another aerial survey of the Wood

Whooping crane

Unlike herons, cranes fly with neck extended.

Buffalo area was made and observers noted two adult cranes and one nest. The previous year's sightings were confirmed. The question then on everybody's lips was: How many birds are there? Soon came word that twenty-eight birds had been counted and, with the three that were then in captivity, the total number of whoopers rose to thirty-one.

By 1964, the number had climbed with painful slowness to fifty birds. Of these, thirty-two were adults, ten were young and eight were in captivity. But in 1974, ten years later, the wild population had only climbed to forty-nine adults and young. Ten birds that had flown to their wintering grounds in Texas in the previous fall had failed to return. What happened to these ten? No one knows; perhaps they had died of natural causes, perhaps they had been gunned down by irresponsible hunters—deliberately, for no one can fail to recognize the majestic bird with the bugle call, the tallest of all our species.

Whoopers, with their long black legs and long necks, stand

about five feet tall and are predominantly white with black wing tips, which are more or less hidden when the wings are folded. They also have a small black patch on the back of the head. Their faces are bare and the skin is red-hued, a pale carmine that extends to give the fairly long yellow beak a slight rosy tint.

Whoopers apparently mate for life. They produce only one or two young each year in a circular nest made of marsh vegetation, hardly more than a rough enclosure of weeds and rushes with a hollow in the center. Here the brown eggs are laid, and incubated by both parent birds. About thirty-five days later, the ungainly chicks are born and, soon after, begin to move about on their long legs. The youngsters are at first dressed in warm, brownish-yellow down. Later they acquire plumage similar to the adults, but their necks are splashed with rusty brown and their faces are fully feathered.

In the fall, the whoopers rise from their northern breeding grounds and flap away, on wings that span seven feet, to travel to their winter home in Aransas National Wildlife Refuge, southeast of San Antonio, Texas. During this flight, the whoopers can average as much as 200 miles a day, traveling at speeds of up to forty-five miles an hour.

Whooping cranes have enormous, curled windpipes that allow them to produce their thrilling bugle calls: *kerloo, ker-lee-oo.* The magnificent sound of these great birds, so perilously close to extinction, echoes forlornly in the northern wilderness or in the shelter of their coastal home.

Photo Credits

Index

L.J.K.